Doors
to the Sacred

*Everyday Events
as Hints of the Holy*

Bridget Haase, OSU

Sister Bridget Haase, OSU

PARACLETE PRESS

BREWSTER, MASSACHUSETTS

2014 First Printing

Doors to the Sacred: Everyday Events as Hints of the Holy

ISBN: 978-1-61261-476-2

Library of Congress Cataloging-in-Publication Data:
Haase, Bridget, 1942-
  Doors to the sacred : everyday events as hints of the holy / Bridget Haase, OSU.
    pages cm
  ISBN 978-1-61261-476-2 (trade pb)
  1. Devotional literature. 2. Spiritual life—Catholic Church. I. Title.
  BV4832.3.H325 2013
  242—dc23   2013026070

10 9 8 7 6 5 4 3 2 1

Published by Paraclete Press
Brewster, Massachusetts
www.paracletepress.com
Printed in the United States of America

Doors
to the Sacred

Lovingly dedicated to
the residents, staff, and volunteers
of The Boston Home,
DORCHESTER, MASSACHUSETTS,
whose lives each day are
hints of the holy

CONTENTS

DOORS TO THE SACRED
Everyday Events as Hints of the Holy

You Never Know What You'll Find Behind a Closed Door

WHEN I WAS ELEVEN YEARS OLD, MY FAMILY moved from a small home on Cedar Drive in the New Orleans suburbs to a rambling old house on Dupre Street in the city neighborhood called Uptown. The winding front steps, the backyard banana trees occasionally laden with fruit, and my very own room charmed me. I thought that this was a castle in the Haases' kingdom.

What fascinated me was the dark basement, reached by a steep flight of stairs. Steam pipes hung low, hissing and clanging, providing their own sense of mystery. But what I loved to investigate most were the many doors of different widths, heights, and kinds of wood. Most led nowhere, not even to closets; they were just ornamental doors opening to a blank wall. But, in my young imagination, I expected that someday I would open one up to a land of princes and princesses or at least a pirate's treasure.

When I mentioned to my mother how much fun I had opening the basement doors, she, chuckling, encouraged me by replying, "Well, you just *never* know what you'll find behind a closed door." Thinking that Mama may have known something I didn't, I kept my hopes high for months, always anticipating an exciting discovery.

Think of this book as I thought of my basement: an opportunity to open fifty-two doors. Spend a year with *Doors to the Sacred*, if you can. Take your time. One chapter a week will keep you busy, I promise.

Or, use it as a devotional at a weekend retreat or on a day of intensive reflection. Wherever you are along your pilgrim way, I hope you will pray with it before Mass, in Eucharistic adoration, or in a faith formation group. Share it with a friend in a retirement center or in a nursing home, as you commute to work, or in your car as you wait to pick up children from school.

Join me in opening doors to the sacred in our everyday life. Let this book become part and parcel of your daily prayer during the forty days of Lent as you contemplate the mystery of Christ's suffering and death. Recall Resurrection "alleluia" moments in your life during the joyful fifty days of Easter. Reflect on the stories and passages from Scripture during Ordinary Time as you continue your journey of transformation begun in Lent. During the Advent and Christmas seasons, use it as a guidebook as you anticipate and celebrate the coming of Christ in history, mystery, and majesty.

Whenever and wherever you begin, let me offer you a tried and true method for using this book. *The first step* is to descend the steep stairs down into your heart. Select a spiritual trait from the table of contents, open wide the sacred door, and attentively read the story. Walk slowly around the room of the reflection. Although these are my own stories,[1] they can offer you a glimpse of God's presence in *your* life if you take time to see similarities; focus on their perspective; study them from different angles.

Step two is to consider completing during the week, either in your journal or in your heart, the three sentences that follow each story. Please remember that they are meant to be guides to foster thought and help you open your life to grace.

Step three is to ponder the prayers, Scripture passages, or quotes from a saint or holy person that will encourage you to grow in the particular spiritual disposition.

In whatever liturgical season you use this book, I hope you discover that your own hallowed portals reveal hints of the holy in everyday events and lead you into the provident hands of God and the unconditional love of Christ.

Bridget Haase, OSU
November 1, 2013
Feast of All Saints

---

1. Names and some details have been changed.

1

A Part in the Play
Enthusiasm

EIGHT-YEAR-OLD ADELAIDE HAD HER HEART SET on a part in the school play. Running to the car after school, she jumped in, winded and excited. "Look, Mommy," she breathlessly said. "Here are the lines for our class play. It's all about a vegetable garden, fuzzy rabbits, and a bunch of nice neighbors. I am *dying* to be the carrot. She even wiggles when she's pulled up and gets to say a poem about being healthy and sweet." Adelaide chattered all the way home as her mother sank deeper and deeper into the driver's seat.

Paula, Adelaide's patient mother, knew from experience that her daughter did not have much of a chance. She lacked stage presence and struggled to memorize the simplest lines. Each year tryouts resulted in a disappointed child, embarrassed at her inability to be chosen for even the smallest part.

For the next week, Adelaide practiced and practiced the carrot poem. Paula coaxed her and crossed her fingers, constantly anxious that her precious daughter would fail again. Paula wondered why Adelaide couldn't retain a mere nine words: "pointed hats, upside down, growing deeply in the ground." But she was determined not to abandon hope.

The day of tryouts Paula worried and fretted as she prepared her "maybe next time" speech. She visualized the scene as she vacuumed and washed dishes: Adelaide sobbing dramatically and she trying to console her with Fruit Loops and lots of hugs.

At 2:50 PM, Paula drove up to the school, joined the line of cars for after-school pick-up, and, once again, reviewed her pep talk. Taking one long breath, she drove up to the school carport. From the dismissal line Adelaide came jumping and running. She bolted into the car, panting with excitement. "Mommy!," she shouted at the top of her lungs. "I got the best part ever in the *whole* play. I'm *sooo* happy. I get to clap and cheer!"

Paula, breathing a sigh of relief and whispering a prayer of thanks, blew Adelaide happy kisses. Paula knew what "clapping and cheering" meant. Her daughter would be hidden behind the curtain applauding her classmates after each act. But that didn't matter. Adelaide's dream had *finally* come true. She was, at long last, on stage!

Oftentimes we too have our hearts set on a particular job, promotion, or special recognition after years of faithful service. But someone else gets the step-up-the-ladder position we strived for, the salary increase, or the prized trophy at the annual awards dinner. The roles we desire in life never seem to come our way, no matter how much we rehearse, no matter how diligently we work. Watching from the wings, we can allow discouragement to set in as others take center stage, receiving both the applause and the standing ovations.

Part of our mission may well be lauding the success of others. This does not mean that we abandon our desires or personal goals but that we put aside our disappointments to support and praise others' efforts and accomplishments. In so doing, we may discover that clapping for friends and colleagues energizes us, cheering them on brings us selfless happiness and, although we are hidden behind the curtains, lets us discover joy in our part in life's play.

Owning the Story, Opening to Grace

- My role in life is . . .

- It's difficult to clap and cheer for others when . . .

- This week I will praise a colleague or family member with whom I feel in competition by . . .

GOD OF MY LIFE, you "have fashioned me to do some definite service; have committed some work to me which is not committed to another. I have my mission. I may never know it in this life, but I shall be told it in the next. I have a part in a great work; I am a link in a chain, a bond of connection between persons" (John Henry Newman).

Keep on looking up towards the goal you have in view.
Keep on at the task God has given you to do.

(Anonymous)

2

Bargain Hunting
Devotion

FIRST NOTICED HER IN THE TOY SECTION OF THE local Goodwill store. She would choose a stuffed animal or a fire truck, examine it closely, and then, with a pronounced smile of satisfaction, place it in her shopping cart. Hunting for just the right bargain and singing along with the piped Christmas carol, she went up and down each row of each section of the store with both determination and deliberation, selecting items here and there. She eventually parked her full cart in an out-of-the-way corner and got a second one to continue her search. After about an hour, she maneuvered both carts to the checkout counter.

"That will be all together $102.67," said the cashier.

"What do you know!" the shopper exclaimed. "I have a Christmas gift for all seventeen of my grandchildren, and I kept to my $120 limit. I am going home a happy woman."

She put one cart in front of the other and began pushing both of them simultaneously. Realizing it was a bad idea, she both sighed aloud and prayed, "Jesus, help me."

"May I help you?" I asked.

"Mercy me," she said, chuckling. "I call upon the name of the Lord and he comes right to my aid."

I took one cart and she the other as we made our way to the parking lot. She loosened the rope that kept the trunk of her rust-eaten, paint-chipped red Ford tightly closed. As I handed her the bagged purchases, she carefully arranged each one in a secure place.

Out of the blue she blurted, "I have a question for you."

Thinking this interesting woman would ask *my* name as I hoped to ask *hers*, I had "Bridget" on the tip of my tongue. But she had another thought on her mind.

"Tell me, what titles do you use for Jesus?" Before I could even gather my thoughts for an answer, she jumped in. "Me? I love Savior, Deliverer, Prince of Peace, Messiah, King of Kings, and, best of all, just plain Brother. There are so many names to choose from. It just makes me smile."

She jerked open her stubborn car door, settled down in her well-worn driver's seat, and fastened her seat belt. Starting the car, she said in utmost sincerity, "Thanks so much for the help. I hope *you* are going home a happy woman."

Then, leaning out the window to the tune of her chugging engine, she offered goodbye counsel: "Now don't forget to call on the name of the Lord."

In her simple question, spirited response, and prayerful exhortation, a grandmother, bargain hunting in a Goodwill store, offered priceless gifts to me on a cold December day.

Owning the Story, Opening to Grace

- One name of Jesus that has special meaning for me is . . .
- One way I help others respectfully utter the name of Jesus is . . .
- This week I will pray to Jesus as my . . .

O JESUS CHRIST, teach me reverence and devotion as I meditate on your many names. You are my Redeemer who, at the last, will stand upon the earth (Job 19:25), the Wonderful Counselor and Prince of Peace upon whose shoulders authority rests (Isa. 9:6); the Messiah, Emmanuel, who is "God-with-us" (Matt. 1:23); and the Lamb of God, our Savior, who takes away the sin of the world (John 1:29). May I stand before you in wonder and awe, for you are the Son of God (Lk. 1:32). May I also stand before you humbly and confidently, approaching you in utter trust and faithful love, for *you* have called *me* by the name of friend (John 15:15). Amen.

" *God confides his name to those who believe in him; he reveals himself to them in his personal mystery. The gift of a name belongs to the order of trust and intimacy.* **"**

(*Catechism of the Catholic Church*, 2143)

3

Blessing and Inconvenience
Present Moment

RMA LOUISE, A STRONG APPALACHIAN WOMAN, rises early and offers the prayer she has said each morning for sixty-three years: "Thank you, Lord, for another beautiful day to come to me. I'll be a-lookin' for you in every moment." Her seasons are spent in the routine of daily mountain life: tending a fire, drawing water at the well, pickling her garden cucumbers, and going to church. As the gospel radio strains of "Me and God, we got our own thing going, we got it all worked out" drift into the mountain air, Irma Louise knows that living in the present moment is a blessing.

Farther north in Green Bay, Wisconsin, Sean Herriott, a talk show host on the Catholic Relevant Radio Network, also rises early with a prayer to live in the "here and now." His life brims with many hectic demands: hosting a daily four-hour radio program, arranging and hosting guests, accepting last-minute schedule changes and unexpected cancellations, and balancing

▪ A Story

family responsibilities with his career. "Living in the present moment can be tough and really inconvenient," he once shared on the air. Having experienced that no two days, no two hours, will be exactly alike, Sean knows that living in the present moment can be a challenge.

The key to living in the here and now is *awareness* of what we are doing and *acceptance* of what is going on beyond the surface of appearances. This daily discipline is difficult and takes practice. It requires that we be sensitive to what we are experiencing, accept the person before us without judgment, savor and enjoy what surrounds us, and deal with interruptions and change of plans with grace and peace. When we live fully in the here and now, we reverence the holiness of *each* action of our daily routine. Why? Because we are convinced that this moment is God's ambassador that reveals the divine will for us in the here and now. Generously accepting the present moment, we can then gratefully bow to receive its blessing. After all, "me and God, we got our own thing going," right here, right now.

Owning the Story, Opening to Grace

- ▪ I am challenged to live in the present moment when . . .
- ▪ The blessings that are flowing right here, right now are . . .
- ▪ I can reverence the holiness of my daily routine by . . .

GOD, PRESENT IN EACH MOMENT OF MY
DAILY ROUTINE, quiet my heart and saturate me with
your grace right here, right now, as I pray, "Give us this day our
daily bread" (Matt. 6:11). "So do not worry about tomorrow"
(Matt. 6:34). "It is the Lord!" (John 21:7). "Get up . . . and you
will be told what you are to do" (Acts 9:6). "Jesus Christ is the
same yesterday and today and forever" (Heb. 13:8).

❝ *Each day is unique and blessed. There are cloudy days
and sunny; windy, wet days and calm, dry days. It's the
same way with your life. There are ups and downs; no two
days, no two hours, no two moments, are exactly alike.* ❞

(Francis de Sales)

4

Burdens and Rest
Suffering

RADIATING THE QUIET SERENITY OF A LIFE
dedicated to his parish community, elderly Father Michael
Joseph, with conviction and assurance, called us forth. It
was the moment in the Good Friday service to approach the
crucifix and honor it by touch or kiss.

A Story

"My good people," he began. "Come to kiss the cross, yes, but bring your tears and struggles with you. On this holy day thank Jesus for what he has done for you, but also renew your desire to accept the cross in your own life. With great hope and expectation, draw near to the crucifix, and offer your crosses back to Christ, assured that you will find rest."

Slowly the parishioners made their way to the front of the altar. As sobering peace filled the church, we reverenced the cross of Christ and the many other crosses borne on different shoulders.

Life is a challenge. Across the seas there are typhoons and earthquakes, drought and floods, famine and starving refugees. Across our yards neighbors worry about mortgage payments, loss of jobs, and care of elderly parents. Across our dinner tables we glimpse the struggles of teenagers, the pain of family divisions, and the frustration of misunderstandings. Across our own hearts we discover nagging doubts about faith, anxiety about the future, or dissatisfaction for years squandered in selfishness. We feel that life is just too tough, and our crosses, consuming the energy of our hearts, weigh heavily upon our shoulders. We are at a loss as to what to do.

Christ, understanding our struggles, extends a divine invitation: to come to him with all the cares and pains that burden us; with the physical suffering that depletes our strength; and with our spiritual restlessness and confusion. Jesus does not promise to take our worries and cares away or make them disappear. He reminds us that we, like him, will always have crosses to carry, but we never have to bear them alone. In letting Christ help us, in allowing Christ to carry them with us, our crosses will seem lighter upon our shoulders and our hearts will be at rest.

Owning the Story, Opening to Grace

■ The cross that I need to accept is . . .

■ The comforting words of Jesus that bring me rest are . . .

■ My life is full of hope and promise because . . .

CHRIST, COMFORT OF THE AFFLICTED AND BURDENED, "there are days when the burdens we carry chafe our shoulders and wear us down; when the road seems dreary and endless, the skies gray and threatening; when our lives have no music in them and our hearts are lonely, and our souls have lost their courage. Flood the path with light, we beseech you; turn our eyes to where the skies are full of promise" (Augustine of Hippo).

Come to me, all you that are weary and are carrying heavy burdens, and I will give you rest. Take my yoke upon you, and learn from me; for I am gentle and humble in heart, and you will find rest for your souls. For my yoke is easy, and my burden is light.

(Matt. 11:28–30)

5

By My Side
Fidelity

T WAS ALWAYS EASY TO ROUND UP MY SAN ANTONIO, Texas, first graders at the end of noon recess. In fact, they began to line up, to my amazement, about three minutes before the sound of the bell. After a few weeks, I realized why.

Each afternoon after lunch, my students gathered on the floor around my feet for "story time," a favorite ritual that sparked various conversations and an abundance of happy smiles. These six-year-olds discovered that being the first in line yielded a prime place close to the teacher, the book, and the pictures!

This particular day I had chosen one of my favorite books, Robert Munsch's *Love You Forever*, a story of the enduring love of a mother for her son through all his toddler antics, teenage challenges, and other life stages. I had practiced reading the story to myself several times, since experience had taught me that I had never mastered getting through it without a tear or two. As the children bubbled with anticipation, I took a deep breath and began to read. All went well until the very end when the son takes his frail, elderly mother into his arms. As he rocks her, he sings, "I'll love you forever," the song *she* has sung to *him* all through his life. At that moment, tears began to cascade down my face, flooding my eyes as the children, sitting in stunned silence, became one big blur.

Suddenly, I felt a tug on my shoulder. Beside me stood Juan, his little face squinched up in concern and sympathy. He handed me a Kleenex and a gentle hug at the same time. Then, in a tender voice, he comforted me. "Don't cry, Sister. No matter what, I'm always here for you."

Juan gifted me with a compassionate assurance, a promise of faithful love, a pledge to be by my side . . . so like our God.

Owning the Story, Opening to Grace

- ▪ I witness to God's faithful love when I . . .
- ▪ A time I was there for another was . . .
- ▪ In trust and confidence, I ask for the grace this week to . . .

O EVER-FAITHFUL, LOVING GOD,

You are with me when I surrender to your will and when I struggle to accept it.

You are with me in sapphire-sky days and in cloudy futures.

You are with me in the seasons of luscious strawberries and of falling autumn leaves.

You are with me in my mountaintop prayer moments and in my inner valleys of darkness.

You are with me in both the challenges and the comforts of
family life.

You are with me when love for you fills my heart to the brim
and when I struggle to believe.

You are with me when I am called to comfort another and when
I am the one who needs help.

With a grateful heart I thank you for always being there for me
and for loving me unconditionally and forever. Amen.

“ For the LORD is good;
his steadfast love endures forever,
and his faithfulness to all generations. ”
(Ps. 100:5)

6

Called by Name
Affirmation

Y OU KNOW MY NAME!" PETER BLURTED OUT.
"Sure do," I replied. "I love the name and, besides, another Peter is a good friend of mine."

Known to be aloof and gruff, Peter's tone of voice and intimidating manner accompanied his slovenly appearance, a blue secondhand shirt and calloused feet shod in flip-flops. I was so surprised that simply calling him by name steered my acquaintance with this neighbor, who was unfriendly, brusque, and perhaps chronically depressed, in a new direction.

Since moving into low-income housing, I had learned much about sixty-year-old Peter. He could neither read nor write; could not sign his name; and numbers were simply scrambled shapes in his head. He had lost a mentally ill mother when she walked into oncoming traffic; a sister died from severe depression and, two months later, his brother, through unrelenting grief. "I gotta do the best I can," Peter told me. "So these things don't come over me and make me sad."

One autumn morning he stopped me on my way to work. "Got a minute, Sister?" he asked, not knowing my name.

"Every day has twenty-four hours so I've got lots of minutes," I laughingly replied. "What can I do for you?"

"I have this splinter in my foot. Can you take it out? My foot's not too clean so I hope you don't mind. I've been meaning to wash it but I'm always too busy. I have some tweezers here."

Peter propped his smelly foot on a table in the lobby of our apartment building and the digging began. "The tweezers are awful rusty, Peter. I have to be careful so your foot doesn't get infected."

"Aw, I took pain all my life. I certainly can take it now. Don't worry. I won't sue you for malpractice." His belly laugh filled the room.

As I pried the nagging sliver from his foot, I wished I could have removed all the darkness that enveloped him.

The next morning Peter was at the door to thank me. He mentioned that, since he could walk painlessly now, he was headed to Boston's Logan Airport to check the price of tickets to Ireland. He decided it was time to do some traveling before Ole Man Winter iced the roads. I wished him safe travels, a good price for a ticket, and the pleasure of dreams.

I don't know where Peter went that day. I only know that thirty-six hours later he was found beside his motorcycle, his pride and joy, twenty-five feet down a rural ravine. There were no skid marks, no wallet with an ID, and no plane ticket to Ireland. Just a man who steered his motorcycle off the road. It took hours before the police could identify him by name.

Owning the Story, Opening to Grace

- I offered another the gift of recognition and acceptance when . . .

- A name I need to utter in a respectful and peaceful tone of voice is . . .

- I will make the effort this week to learn the name of . . .

GOD, WHO GENTLY CALLS ME BY NAME, GRANT ME THE GRACE TO KINDLY:

Honor your holy Name by speaking it with reverence and devotion and never in frustration or anger.

Learn the names of those who fill my prescriptions, bag my groceries, deliver my mail.

Pray for the nameless victims of war, no matter which side they were on.

Bless in my heart those whose names I will never know but who try desperately to survive.

Offer prayers for those who die alone with no one to identify their bodies.

Thank you for knowing my name and speaking it with unconditional love until you call me home.

I pray this in the glorious Name of our Savior, Jesus Christ, for whom every head should bow. Amen.

> *But now thus says the LORD,*
> *he who created you, O Jacob,*
> *he who formed you, O Israel:*
> *Do not fear, for I have redeemed you;*
> *I have called you by name, you are mine.*
>
> (Isa. 43:1)

7

Catching Fire
Witness

HAVE MY FIFTH GRADERS REALLY GRASPED *the events of Pentecost?* I asked myself as I prepared the final religion exam of the school year. I thought about Jesus's disciples huddled in fear in a locked room and my students, gazing out of windows and chomping at the bit for that first baseball pitch. I'd know soon enough, I mused, as they retold the story in their own words.

Correcting my students' papers later in the week, I smiled as I glanced at Kaylee's storytelling. All year I had enjoyed this twelve-year-old's presence in my class, her exuberance popping out from hazel eyes framed in fashionable glasses. Her insights were quite impressive even though she took words quite literally. So I was not surprised when I read her sincere and simple interpretation of the scriptural reference to the "tongues, as of fire" (Acts 2:3).

Kaylee began her account of Pentecost (Acts 2:1–3) with the facts: the day came; the apostles were together in one place; a sound like the rush of wind came from heaven, filling the house. "But what *really* happened at Pentecost," she wrote, "was that the apostles' tongues began to burn, flames came off their lips, they ran into the streets with open mouths, and everybody caught Jesus fire."

Each Pentecost since then, I have wondered what life would be like if we all caught Jesus fire: to live in the warmth of surrender to God's will and in service of others. Perhaps we would reach out even more to those smoldering in the ashes of shame, rejection, and self-destructive behavior. Maybe we would fan flames of potential, possibility, and passion even as we accepted the demands of the present moment. Certainly our hands and hearts would hold torches of integrity, justice, and peace. And, to be sure, a flame of love would impel us to serve the homeless, the hungry, the powerless, and those forgotten and abandoned. Catching Jesus fire together, spark by spark, would create a raging bonfire and set the world ablaze. As Kaylee taught me in her own way, this is the invitation and fulfillment of Pentecost.

Owning the Story, Opening to Grace

■ I caught Jesus fire when someone . . .

■ I bring fire to this earth each time I . . .

■ In trust and confidence, I ask for the grace this week to . . .

O HOLY SPIRIT, blow on the embers of our souls and ignite your Pentecostal fire within us. One with you and united to the family of every nation and race, may we all catch Jesus fire. May we live in surrender to your will and give our lives in service to others. Enkindle understanding, compassion, and faith within us. May these sparks of love then leap from heart to heart until the whole world is ablaze and Pentecost comes again. Amen.

" I came to bring fire to the earth, and how I wish it were already kindled! "

(Lk. 12:49)

8

Change and Exchange
Sensitivity

A Story

RACING TO BE ON TIME TO MEET MY FRIEND for lunch, I hurried past a newspaper vendor, his authorized blue badge glistening in the sun. "*Spare Change* newspaper, folks. New edition! Help the homeless," he cried.

Spare Change News is a twenty-year-old fixture on Boston street corners. This newspaper's state goal is to show "that the homeless, with the proper resources and opportunity, create change for themselves by striving for self-sufficiency." Homeless men and women purchase each copy for twenty-five cents, sell it for one dollar, and keep the profit. But, even more, the sale of *Spare Change News* is an unspoken invitation to greet the vendors, to acknowledge their presence, to compassionately approach them as a brother or a sister.

Passersby will certainly pause, chat, and purchase a paper. It's such a noble and established project, I thought. *Bet he'll get lots of takers.* I didn't think twice about not stopping and bolting across the street to the café.

My friend Mary Jo and I caught up with each other in the crowded eatery. Finally finding a free table in front of wide windows, we had an exciting view of bustling street activity. There were men in long black woolen coats lugging briefcases, well-heeled and high-heeled women carrying brown bags and wrapped salads, and mothers with strollers bulging with both infants and discount store shopping bags. My eye also spied the homeless man energetically hawking his newspapers next to a city trash receptacle.

What astounded me was that, during our forty-five-minute lunch, no one bought a newspaper, greeted this street person, or even acknowledged his presence. They simply passed him by, walking as fast as they could on their way to more important things.

"How," I asked Mary Jo, "can people ignore someone trying to better himself? What can be more important than sharing a little extra or extending a pleasant greeting? It wouldn't take long, so why don't passersby do it? What's the big rush? Why don't they have the time?"

Listening sympathetically to my barrage of harsh judgments, Mary Jo waited patiently for me to come up for air. Then, looking me straight in the eye, she gently challenged, "Did you?"

Owning the Story, Opening to Grace

■ When I give change to a poor person, coupled with a kind exchange, I learn that . . .

■ Sometimes I race past a street person because . . .

■ I ask for the grace this week to help someone in need by . . .

O GRACIOUS GOD, WHO NOTICES US AND SPEAKS TO US, let me never disappoint those in need by ignoring their presence through silence or fear. Grant me the grace to approach the poor as brother or sister; to speak to them with gentle empathy; to advance their well-being with generosity; and to assist them in their endeavors to become self-sufficient. May I always take time to offer spare change but, even more, the treasure of an exchange of words filled with encouragement and hope. Amen.

> *Today it is fashionable to talk about the poor. Unfortunately it is not fashionable to talk with them.*
> (Mother Teresa of Calcutta)

9

Collector's Items
Searching

THIS STORY IS NOT MY OWN BUT WAS OFTEN told by Archbishop Fulton J. Sheen to audiences rapt in attention.

"Hi, Mr. Sampson! Whatcha lookin' for?" the curious Jimmy Ray shouted from his first-floor balcony. He would watch his

A Story

neighbor slowly walk up and down the street, turn the corner at the pharmacy, and then disappear into the distance. All the while, Mr. Sampson never looked up, his eyes glued to the ground. So, Jimmy Ray thought, he's got to be collecting some very important things, and he wished he knew what these mysterious items were.

This day a high-pitched voice interrupted Jimmy Ray's thoughts. "Well, son," Mr. Sampson answered with head still bent, "once I found a dollar bill. Not really sure what I am looking for but never know what I might find."

Jimmy Ray felt sorry for Mr. Sampson, walking with his head down, back hunched over. He missed the beauty of cloud formations in azure skies, the heart-shaped leaves of the linden trees in the local park, and even the brightly colored purple slide and neon green swings on the renovated neighborhood playground.

The years passed. Mr. Sampson never abandoned his everyday quest, his search for "whatever," even as stiff knees and poor health slowed him down. If only he kept seeking, he convinced himself, he would one day find what he was looking for. He never thought that his daily practice would abruptly end.

Only a handful of people attended Mr. Sampson's wake and burial. Beside the single bouquet of orange and yellow chrysanthemums from City Councilor Jimmy Ray were three glass jars: one with innumerable buttons, paperclips, and safety pins; another jar with about 650 pennies and a few nickels, dimes, and quarters; and a third that was three-fourths filled with dollar bills and several fives. "Search, and you will find" (Matt.7:7), read the simple sign that told of a lifetime of day-after-day treasure hunts, shoe gazing, and an aching back.

"Mr. Sampson's entire life's search was reduced to three jars filled with trifles," concluded Archbishop Sheen. Then, with compelling urgency, he paused and poignantly challenged us. "Life will always be a questing. What are you spending *your* years looking for?"

Owning the Story, Opening to Grace

- What I am really looking for in life is . . .
- The superficial things that distract me on my search are . . .
- I have already discovered the worth of . . .

GOD OF MY SEEKING, rekindle in me a true search for you:

When I look for you in all the wrong places or in countless meaningless things.

When I am restless and my heart is empty.

When I collect wrongs done to me or tally up life's unfair challenges.

When I am so preoccupied with myself and miss the songs of birds and the rustle of autumn leaves.

When I am confused and do not even know what I am seeking.

When I am convinced that I have found you.

> ❝ *It is God for whom we are looking. Unhappiness is due not to a want of something **outside** us, but to a want of something **inside** us. No wonder everything short of God disappoints us.* ❞
> (Fulton J. Sheen)

10

Encounters and Connections
Community

"SISTER, HERE'S A SEAT. THERE'S PLENTY OF ROOM," I said, motioning a welcome. Sister smiled, ambled over, and sat down with a little sigh. We had never met, so I introduced myself and she did the same. We were exchanging a few pleasantries when the bell chimed to begin Morning Prayer.

Before heading to a seminar on women mystics that we were both attending, we lingered to continue our introductions. I shared a little bit about myself and my ministry at The Boston Home.

When I finished, Sister Joanne McMahon quietly commented, "I have just retired."

Curious, I asked this Maryknoll missionary sister if her service had been in the United States or abroad. Sister Joanne smiled and said, "It was abroad in a place you probably have never heard of. I was missioned to the island of Yap, Micronesia."

Stunned, I said, "Sister Joanne, I *have* heard of Yap. Would you, by any chance, know a Jesuit priest by the name of Father John Mulreany? He's teaching in a small Catholic high school there."

With equal amazement, Sister Joanne lit up. "Of course I know Father John! I worked with him in the school. His mother and sister Jennifer visited the island last February. Would you know *them?*"

"I *do* know them," I enthusiastically replied, astounded that a brief introductory conversation with a stranger became a global connection.

"How did you find out about Yap and the high school?" asked Sister Joanne.

I recounted how Jennifer, who had come to The Boston Home three years earlier to assist in filming a segment for *NBC Nightly News* with Brian Williams, happened to mention that her brother was a Jesuit seminarian finishing his studies at nearby Boston College. Over the months that followed, Jennifer kept me posted on her brother's priestly ordination, his being missioned to Yap, and her and her mother's planned February visit.

Having returned from her trip, Jennifer shared photos of myriad aspects of life on the island: the constructing of the three-room school through the generous and hard manual labor of the islanders, the efforts of the American volunteer teachers to fulfill the children's dreams for an education, the ceremonies in native dress and traditional celebrations on Yap Day, the abundance of coconuts and its nourishing milk, and even planning the feat of tying down the school before a predicted typhoon.

"But it was more than simply sharing photos or events, Sister Joanne," I said. "This ordinary encounter in Boston, Massachusetts, joined my life to one of the more than six hundred islands of the Federated States of Micronesia and to the ministry of the Jesuits there. It's incredible, isn't it?"

Knowing about this dedicated priest and his colleagues convinced me that all our lives span much bigger horizons than our own space in the world. I know I will never get to Yap, Micronesia. But there is no need to do so, for Yap, through Sister Joanne's years of service, Jennifer's enthusiasm, and Father John's commitment, has come to me.

Owning the Story, Opening to Grace

- ■ I marvel at the invisible lines that join all of us when . . .
- ■ One practical way I can support the work of missionaries around the world is . . .
- ■ This week I will learn more about life in the country of . . .

GOD OF ALL PEOPLES, may I realize with gratitude and commitment that your "various gifts are handed out everywhere; but they all originate in [your] Spirit. [Your] various ministries are carried out everywhere; but they all originate in [your] Spirit. [Your] various expressions of power are in action everywhere; but [you yourself are] behind it all. Each person is given something to do that shows who [you are]: Everyone gets in on it, everyone benefits" (1 Cor. 12:4–7, THE MESSAGE).

    There will be no other sign that you are in the grace of the Lord than that you are united together.

(Angela Merici)

11

Everyday Christmas
Incarnation

SHORTLY AFTER HALLOWEEN, MY MOTHER WOULD haul boxes of Christmas ornaments from our basement. I'd catch her admiring the heirloom, glass-blown decorations or dusting off the crèche. Dinner conversations would drift off to talk of Christmas tree lots and the fragrance of pine needles. Christmas carols and music would drift

A Story

through our home. We would dry dishes to the peaceful strains of "Silent Night" or try to do homework as the refrains of "Joy to the World" put a tap in our feet. Often we slumbered off to "Angels We Have Heard on High."

This anticipation often puzzled and sometimes disturbed me. Our house was always ahead of the Church and not in sync with the liturgical calendar. We skipped Advent! "Mama," I finally asked one evening, "Why do you begin to celebrate Christmas so early?"

"Darlin', why not?" she replied with a certainty born of her deep faith.

Existing before time began, Jesus, in the Incarnation, entered our world in a moment in time. God from on high, he was cradled in Bethlehem and made his home with us. But Jesus did not just *enter* our world; he *became* like us. He reveled in all aspects of human life: from learning his prayers to perfecting a trade; from the demands of duty to relishing solitude; from enlivening conversations with friends to enjoying wedding feasts. In each experience, Jesus taught us how to embrace life: in prayer and hard work; in worries and wonder; in attentive listening and festive celebrations.

Mama had it right. Why not celebrate the Incarnation with each sunrise? The mystery of Christ's entering our world and our life fits any season. Rejoicing each day in the marvel of Emmanuel, God-with-us, we can sing for joy with the angels in the morning and calmly embrace every silent night. And in between go tell it on the mountain that the Lord has come.

Owning the Story, Opening to Grace

▨ I proclaim and celebrate that the Lord has come among us by . . .

▨ I embrace life as Jesus did when . . .

▨ I experience the saving power of God when . . .

CHRIST, INCARNATE WORD OF GOD, PRESENT AMONG US, ALL THE ENDS of the earth have seen your saving power. "O sing to the LORD a new song,

for he has done marvelous things.

His right hand and his holy arm

have gotten him victory.

The LORD has made known his victory;

he has revealed his vindication in the sight of the nations.

He has remembered his steadfast love and faithfulness

to the house of Israel.

All the ends of the earth have seen

the victory of our God.

Make a joyful noise to the LORD, all the earth;

break forth into joyous song and sing praises."

(Ps. 98:1–4)

> *Celebrate the feast of Christmas every day, even every moment, in the interior temple of your spirit where you will be reborn each moment in the Divine Word, Jesus Christ.*
> (Paul of the Cross)

12

Father and Daughter
Strength

WORDS, LIKE SEEDS SOWN, CAN TAKE ROOT, grow, and fragrantly blossom. I discovered this a few weeks after leading a women's retreat in Illinois. Lori Vitek, a young woman in Wauconda, Illinois, picked the flowers of my thoughts and sent me this touching bouquet.

Dear Sister Bridget,

Thank you for leading our women's February retreat. It was nice to have time away from my daily routine to share faith-filled moments with others who seek to walk in the Spirit. I would like to share the power and the grace of six words that you spoke with conviction and passion: "We are more than our bodies." These words have made a permanent home within my heart as I think of my dad.

You see, I was the daughter of a special needs father. As a young child, I didn't see my father, Paul Decker, as being different. He was just my father. I knew that he struggled physically: jerking, wincing, hanging onto the walls when he would walk inside the house. Eventually I watched him operate a scooter, maneuvering tight corners and small spaces the best he could. But his ability to so completely love my mom and me outshined the darkness of his physical reality, as did his faith in God.

Dad's prayer, after marrying my mother, was to be blessed with a daughter. After sustaining multiple injuries as a marine in Vietnam (even receiving the Purple Heart!), Dad was afraid he wouldn't have the physical ability to play ball and roughhouse with a boy. His prayer was answered and, in turn, God blessed *me* with a wonderful father.

Oh, the fun we had! Fried chicken picnics, tic-tac-toe and breadsticks at our favorite pizza hangout, taking me to the town's sledding hill and watching, cold but happily enjoying my giddy joy, from inside his Mercury Comet.

Over the years, Dad and I talked about faith; he dried my teenage tears; and with just one loving touch of his hand he could cast out sadness and fear from my heart.

Five years prior to his death, Dad was diagnosed with mitochondrial myopathy. This illness did its best to have its way with him, but my father always found ways to prevail. His spastic hands managed to hold perfectly steady with each embrace he gave me. Those warm, healing hands could comfort fellow nursing home residents living with Alzheimer's who would otherwise lash out at anyone who came near.

His body weakened. But illness could not crush his spirit, silence his wise words, or extinguish his steadfast faith. Even as pain shot through his body, Dad offered consoling words to roommates and lonely souls who had nothing but his selfless fellowship.

A heroic warrior in every sense, my father prayerfully chose to face the challenges in his life with a disciplined courage and steadfast love for others. He desired to show Jesus's love to all he encountered. That love blazes today like an eternal flame within my soul. I am comforted and convinced that every kindness I am able to offer others first began as a seed within my father's very able and abiding heart. He planted it within me and now waters it and watches it grow.

Indeed, my father was so much more than his body. *Indeed,* his legacy of love lives on. When the challenges in my own life seem unsurpassable, I am reminded in the hush of a heavenly whisper that I know comes from Dad that I can do all things, just as he did, through Christ who loves and strengthens me.

With gratitude, Lori

Owning the Story, Opening to Grace

▪ The personal hurdles that challenge me are . . .

▪ I can draw strength from those who overcome physical and emotional obstacles by . . .

▪ I claim the power of my human spirit when I . . .

GOD OF POWER AND MIGHT, may these words become alive within our hearts and bring us hope in times of distress. "So we do not lose heart. Even though our outer nature is wasting away, our inner nature is being renewed day by day. For this slight momentary affliction is preparing us for an eternal weight of glory beyond all measure, because we look not at what can be seen but at what cannot be seen; for what can be seen is temporary, but what cannot be seen is eternal" (2 Cor. 4:16–18). Amen.

May you be made strong with all the strength that comes from his glorious power, and may you be prepared to endure everything with patience.

(Col. 1:11)

13

Fields of Hope
Dreams

IL' WILLIAM, SON OF BIG WILLIAM, HAS WORKED in the Kentucky fields since the age of five. He has an ongoing love affair with the land.

Lil' William's days, at age twelve, follow the planting and harvesting routine with extra sleep and a bit of schooling snatched during off-seasons. He rises early, preferring the cool morning hours and the feel of damp soil under his bare feet. But he takes the heat of the day in stride. "No sun, no crops, no money, no food," he says, sweating and flashing stained teeth. The land has become part and parcel of who he is. With pride he'll point to his harvest, tobacco leaves hanging in the barn to dry.

With a disabled father and six siblings, family responsibilities weigh heavily upon this child's shoulders. But adult thoughts of the future dance in his young mind. "The land is my friend," Lil' William told me one sultry summer evening, "and someday I'll buy a few acres and do my own plantin' and harvestin'. Make myself my own boss with a better life. No matter what, nobody can take away this dream." He is a child of hope and a little man with a big plan.

We are also children of hope with master plans. But the future is both a challenge and a mystery. Until it is upon us, it keeps the secret of all the crossroads and detours of our journeys. We can never be sure when the earth will shift under our feet, when our goals will sway, or our dreams totter.

But nurturing hope always grounds and sustains us. It opens us to potential and possibility, fosters undying dreams, stirs up passion for what lies ahead, and keeps us putting one foot in front of the other. Clinging to hope, Lil' William will one day set his feet in fertile acres; and we will plant ours in the Promised Land.

Owning the Story, Opening to Grace

■ Hope grounds and sustains me when . . .

■ Dreams that open me to potential and possibility are . . .

■ I face the future in trust and with passion because . . .

O GOD, AWAKE TO MY DREAMS, stir up my passion for the future and keep hope alive within my heart. Grant me the grace to realize that you are a God of expectation and possibility. I truly can feel the potential under my feet because I believe that hope is stronger than any fear that overcomes me. In your divine goodness grant me the courage to go forth with hope for what is possible, with excitement for what lies ahead, and with diligent toil for making my dreams come true. Amen.

Consult not your fears but your hopes and your dreams. Think not about your frustrations, but about your unfulfilled potential. Concern yourself not with what you tried and failed in, but with what it is still possible for you to do.

(Pope John XXIII)

14

Floyd's General Store
Kindness

ON A HOT, STICKY SUMMER DAY, PASSING through a small West Virginia town on my way to Kentucky, I noticed a homemade plywood sign propped on the side of the road: "Good Deals at Floyd's General Store." *Inviting*, I thought. *I'll check it out.*

Entering the general store was like walking into a picture postcard of Appalachian life. The owner, Mr. Floyd Carter, came over to introduce himself, told me to call him "Floyd," and then formally introduced me to his wife, Bessie, a picture of serenity as she comfortably sat on the wooden bench next to the coal stove.

"Stove's awaitin' for winter," said Floyd, "and Bessie is settin' there ready to welcome it!" Bessie laughed, enjoying Floyd's Appalachian sense of humor, which seemed to tickle her like a cat's tail running over her foot.

Looking around I saw some of the advertised good deals: greeting cards that held the dust of several months for twenty-five cents; "never-been-used-before brooms" for three dollars; potato chips "sold only three bags at a time so don't ask for only one" for four dollars; Larry's Peanuts still loose and unbagged in their cardboard cartons; and five handmade quilts, each Saran-Wrapped with an invitation to "give a price for Bessie's work."

As I enjoyed this disappearing slice of American life, I imagined the daily conversations and kindnesses Floyd and Bessie must certainly offer the mountain folks. Suddenly, the tinkling of the little bell on the door jolted me out of my musings.

"Come on in, Gary. Bet you're coming for the usual loaf of bread and cans of Coke."

"I sure am, Floyd. It's awful nice when you know what I want even before I ask. Much obliged."

Turning to greet this customer as West Virginia courtesy demanded, I was totally taken aback. Gary had only half a face. I had never seen this type of deformity and a surge of pity and sadness welled up within me. Gathering control, I extended my hand as I looked straight and strongly into Gary's one eye that radiated kindness.

Floyd, Bessie, and Gary began sharing concerns about the summer dry spell and its effect on the pole beans, tomatoes, and wells; the Lowell family's unemployment; and the church meeting with the new pastor at Saturday night's potluck supper.

After he paid for the loaf of bread and cans of soda, Gary tipped his hat and said goodbye. When he was gone, I turned and asked, "Floyd, how does Gary manage?"

"Manage?" he repeated. "Gary doesn't have time to think about himself, what he's got or doesn't have. He's too busy being kind to other people. That bread and those sodas weren't for him, you know."

On that sweltering July day in Floyd's General Store on a rural road in West Virginia, I met a man with half a face and a five-chambered heart—the extra one for kindness.

Owning the Story, Opening to Grace

■ A loving kindness that always brings a smile to my face is . . .

■ The last time I helped someone in need was . . .

■ A time I looked beyond a person's appearance to the inherent goodness inside was . . .

GOD OF KINDNESS, grant, I beseech you:
That the poor will taste your kindness through my generous works of charity and service.

That those who are exploited will experience your kindness through the work of our civil leaders.

That those who suffer violence will know your kindness through my acts of justice and peace.

That those who are sick and challenged by chronic disease will feel your kindness through all health care workers.

That those who have died may receive eternal life through your divine kindness and overflowing mercy.

❝ *Grant, O Lord, that your grace may always go before me and be ever at my back, keeping me ever intent upon good and kind works to be done, through Jesus Christ, your Son and my Lord.* ❞

(Thomas à Kempis)

15

Gaping Holes and Damaged Bricks
Perfection

CAN WE MEET OVER TEA AND RASPBERRY cream puffs?" asked my former sophomore student Jerry. His out-of-the-blue phone call surprised me. It was twenty years after our time together in high school. He was my adolescent challenge par excellence as a high school

A Story

religion teacher. Jerry belligerently questioned everything, not just in words but also in deeds. Late assignments, if ever done, were accompanied with elaborate excuses, deadlines yielded to open-ended dates, routine academic questions developed into unnecessary peppery debates as to why they had to be answered. With rapid pulse and thumping heartbeat, I would enter the classroom and wonder what Jerry would be up to in the hour that followed.

Socially, Jerry was problematic. He instigated quarrels, disregarded school rules, and challenged every after-school detention. But I knew that he went home to an empty house, to burdensome household tasks that fell to him in his mother's absence due to her second job, and to three siblings that needed nurturing and protective care. I felt helpless and unable to seal his life's gaps or chisel the chip on his shoulder. I watched each day as he climbed the scaffold of daily duties and responsibilities, alone.

In early spring when students' thoughts turned to summer vacation, Jerry's turned to baking. He would treat me to an éclair, a melt-in-your-mouth strudel, or a crusty napoleon. "Made the pastries myself," he would proudly announce. Doubting his honesty, I wondered what bakery he patronized.

Funny how time has a way of erasing the chalkboard. Delighted to see him again, I listened as he offered a rundown of how he had worked through the less-than-honorable years of his youth and his journey to the culinary arts. With a taste of pride dolloped with doubt, Jerry hesitantly announced, "I took my damaged bricks and constructed something good. I must admit that my life is solidly built. But, to be honest, there's one hole that never seems to get puttied and keeps my life less than perfect. So, whether I like it or not, I guess there'll always be work for the Master Builder!"

As Jerry's raspberry cream puff melted in my mouth, I marveled that, twenty years earlier, I had taught an extraordinary pastry chef with exceptional wisdom and a taste for architecture!

Owning the Story, Opening to Grace

▪ One of my personal gaps that never gets caulked is . . .

▪ God's skillful love took my life's damaged bricks and . . .

▪ A special grace I need in order to better my life is . . .

GOD, MASTER BUILDER OF MY LIFE, you alone lay the foundation and complete the work of perfection within me. Grace me with the understanding that "I accomplish only a fraction of the magnificent enterprise that is your work. I may never see the end results but that is the difference between the master builder and the worker. I am a worker, not a master builder. I am a prophet of a future not my own" (Oscar Romero).

" *God alone completes in us the work of perfection. God lays the foundation; begins the first scaffolding; constructs it according to divine measurements; and then finishes it by roofing.* "

(Paulinus of Nola)

16

Gift of Sandals
Generosity

T HE HOLY MAN WAS TRAVELING TO A CITY IN India. Running late due to the crowd of onlookers pressing to see him, Mahatma Gandhi was walking quickly to board the train when his sandal loosened, fell off, and landed on the ground. As he paused and bent over to retrieve it, a poor, barefooted boy spied the sandal, grabbed it tightly, and ran.

Gandhi boarded the train. Sitting next to a window and glancing out, he noticed the youth looking from afar, waving Gandhi's sandal with a sense of satisfaction and delight. Immediately, Gandhi removed the other one from his foot, aimed it in the direction of the boy, and tossed it out the window.

A Story

The friend accompanying Gandhi asked why he had done such a thing since they were the only sandals he owned.

Gandhi replied with humble compassion, "Now he has a pair."

Three hours later, the train pulled into a rainy, slippery station and Gandhi disembarked, barefooted.

Owning the Story, Opening to Grace

■ The spontaneity of Gandhi's gift reminds me of . . .

■ A time I held on to an unnecessary possession that another could use was . . .

■ This week I will give from my need by . . .

SELF-GIVING GOD, give me a free, generous heart that puts these words into practice:

" *And when was it that we saw you a stranger and welcomed you, or naked and gave you clothing?'* . . . *And the king will answer them, 'Truly I tell you, just as you did it to one of the least of these who are members of my family, you did it to me.' (Matt. 25:38–40).* "

He [Jesus] looked up and saw rich people putting their gifts into the treasury; he also saw a poor widow put in two small copper coins. He said, 'Truly I tell you, this poor widow has put in more than all of them; for all of them have contributed out of their abundance, but she out of her poverty has put in all she had to live on.'

(Lk. 21:1–4)

What good is it, my brothers and sisters, if you say you have faith but do not have works? . . . If a brother or sister is naked and lacks daily food, and one of you says to them, 'Go in peace; keep warm and eat your fill,' and yet you do not supply their bodily needs, what is the good of that? So faith by itself, if it has no works, is dead.

(Jas. 2:14–17)

Give all for all; seek nothing; take nothing back that you have given up and then you shall truly possess me.

(Thomas à Kempis)

An ounce of practice is worth more than tons of preaching.

(Mahatma Gandhi)

17

Golden Thread
Caring

J IM ORCUTT AND HIS WIFE, TERRY, WERE SHARING their ministry as cofounders of My Brother's Keeper, a Massachusetts nonprofit agency whose sole mission is to "bring the love and hope of Jesus Christ to those we serve" through food and furniture distribution. In the course of our spirited and encouraging conversation, Jim mused how often God chooses us to be the answer to someone's prayer. It is a golden thread woven into life.

Cornelia was a longtime neighbor, struggling to provide for her family. Her minimum wage job as the window waitress at a fast food chain was hardly enough to feed the eleven family members living with her. She, her disabled husband, and their three small children were already living in a cramped apartment when her aging mother moved in. Several months later, her sister's home was in foreclosure, so she and her husband wondered if Cornelia would "take them and their three children in for a while." This "while" had already been two years. Even pooling limited resources, the extended family scrimped by. Cornelia was seeking nighttime employment with a cleaning company to make up the difference.

Christmas was drawing near when Cornelia came to see me. Her unusual, sheepish demeanor hinted to me that something was wrong. "Sister," she awkwardly began, "I was just wondering if you had any grocery gift cards that I could have to buy some extra food for Christmas Day. I really am at the bottom of the barrel." It was the first time Cornelia had ever asked for help and, much to my chagrin, I had absolutely nothing to offer. I always had to depend on the donations of others to help those in need. Cornelia's understanding eclipsed my personal disappointment, and we wished each other a blessed Christmas.

That afternoon I had an unexpected phone call from a local radio station's marketing person. "Sister, this is Jeanne. You don't know me and we have never met. I have been calling local churches to see if I can help a family at Christmas. No one has even returned my calls. I would love to give some grocery gift cards so that a family could have a special holiday meal. Plus some presents and a tree. Do you know of anyone who could use a boost? And one more thing, I've got a question that's haunting me. Why do you think no one called me back?"

"Jeanne," I exclaimed, "I have *just* the family that could use assistance. *And* I also have a response to your dilemma. There is no doubt in my mind that God saved you for us. God chose you to be the answer to someone's prayer."

Cornelia and her family celebrated Christmas with a brightly decorated tree, with trucks that honked and blinked their lights, with dolls that cooed and smiled, and with turkey, mashed potatoes, and ice cream. Cornelia sang with renewed hope that "the Lord had come." And perhaps she wondered why the Child in the manger had a little golden thread woven into his swaddling clothes.

Owning the Story, Opening to Grace

- I became an answer to someone's prayer when . . .
- Others wove golden threads of help into my life when . . .
- In trust and confidence, I ask for the grace this week to . . .

O CARING CHRIST, I ASK YOU THAT

When a brother stretches out a hand and calls for help, I may be an answer to his prayer.

When a sister hungers for food or an encouraging, consoling word, I may be an answer to her prayer.

When another is suffering and finds it impossible to pray, I may become his or her pray-er.

When life weighs heavily upon my shoulders and I need another to share my burden, someone may weave a golden thread of care and prayer into my life.

All the good that you will do will come not from you but from the fact that you have allowed yourself to be used by God's love. Be more open to the power that will work through you without your knowing it.

(Thomas Merton)

18

Grotto of Massabielle
Pilgrimage

A DREAM I HAD, TO PRAY TO THE BLESSED MOTHER in the hollowed rock in Lourdes, France, was coming true. My Ursuline sisters in Pau, about twenty miles from the Shrine of Our Lady of Lourdes, surprised me with a train ticket to go there on a day's pilgrimage.

Arriving at Lourdes with a wildflower bouquet, I made my way to the grotto of Massabielle. It is the place, hewn from rock, where Mary appeared to Bernadette Soubirous, a French peasant, in 1858.

Entering the grotto in reverence, I thought about the thousands and thousands of sick pilgrims who have come here in hopes of being physically cured or spiritually healed. Discreetly tucking my simple gift into the bouquets of fragrant red roses and vibrant yellow sunflowers, I prayed quickly for an increase of faith, hope, and love. There was no time for lingering since officials kept the line moving briskly!

I have many memories of that May day: strolling along the banks of the glistening Gave River; admiring the majestic mountain peaks of the Pyrenees; watching the sick and disabled being wheeled to the healing baths; praying the rosary at the

Basilica of the Immaculate Conception; and participating in the afternoon procession of the Blessed Sacrament.

But what I remember most vividly is a woman in her late seventies kneeling on the bare ground, oblivious to her surroundings, unpretentious in her posture, and absorbed in prayer. She made no sound, but her lips moved and then stopped; moved again, stopped. As I watched her engage in this spiritual dialogue, I felt a great desire to examine my own prayer. Was I really listening to the Divine, or was I spending my prayer talking and babbling in a one-sided conversation? Did I ever give God time to speak to me?

Boarding the local train to return to Pau, I thanked God for being able to pray along with so many other faith-filled believers. But, more than that, I realized that the Mother of God had encouraged me to *truly* converse with her Son in each moment and event in my life. She had inspired me to replace my rambling monologues with a dialogue. Our Lady of Lourdes had spoken to *me* in the cave of *my* heart through the devotion of a pilgrim who knew the secret of prayer.

Owning the Story, Opening to Grace

- True prayer, for me, is . . .
- I listen to the word of God in the "cave of my heart" when . . .
- I honor the Blessed Mother by . . .

MOTHER OF GOD AND WOMAN OF FAITH, teach us to listen to each moment of our lives in confident trust, receiving the word of God in the cave of our hearts. You are the comforter of the poor, mother of all nations, friend of the lonely, guide of travelers, strength of the weak, and help of the dying. May we know that a seed of hope has been planted within us for, in you, Mother of believers, are light and strength. Holy Mary, Our Lady of Lourdes, pray for us. Amen.

(adapted from the traditional litany of Our Lady of Lourdes)

Immaculate Mary, thy praises we sing;
Who reigns now in splendor with Jesus our King.
In heaven the blessed thy glory proclaim;
On earth, we, thy children, invoke your sweet name.
Thy name is our power, thy virtues our light,
Thy love is our comfort, thy pleading our might.
We pray for our mother, the Church upon earth;
And bless, Holy Mary, the land of our birth.
Ave, ave, ave Maria.
Ave, ave Maria.

(traditional Lourdes hymn)

19

Hot, Steaming Coffee
Acceptance

H IS FACE WAS FAMILIAR, BUT I NEVER KNEW his name. Many times I had passed him on the same street, same corner, in Boston. His belongings were tucked in the same blue canvas duffle bag. His black, torn jacket with its "I visited Colorado" patch hung loosely like a church vestment from another era, his green outdoor mat and brown striped blanket arranged with almost liturgical precision, his broken glasses still unrepaired. But the song he sang was always different. "When You Wish Upon a Star" created a longing in me. "It's a Small, Small World" reminded me that we are responsible for one another. And I could only quietly pray with his rendition of "God Bless America." This street person acted as my pedestrian pastor and preacher.

I reached into my purse to give him some coins as if the basket were being passed. All of a sudden, I noticed that this homeless man was drinking a cup of McDonald's coffee. Zipping my purse closed, I mumbled to myself that he doesn't need my quarters if he has money for fast food and continued my walk to the nearby church. During Mass, my judging conscience chilled my bones, but I defended myself, saying I had been prudent.

After Mass, I retraced my steps. I felt relieved that I did not encounter him again. As I passed McDonald's, a whiff of coffee lured me in like the smell of incense. *A treat*, I thought, *to warm me up and for a week of hard work ahead.* Standing in line, I noticed a familiar black, torn jacket with a dangling patch and realized that the homeless man was in front of me. *I was right*, I thought. *He has money, and I saved myself from being taken advantage of.* I breathed a sigh of self-righteous relief. As he approached the counter, the petite, elderly clerk asked, "A coffee refill?" The man nodded, embarrassingly. Handing him a cup, the clerk told him to stay warm and come back tomorrow. Then that loving senior citizen pulled out a purple-flowered coin purse from her uniform pocket, took out a bill, and rang up the register.

Owning the Story, Opening to Grace

- I am critical of the poor and needy when . . .
- I surprised someone with a big-hearted gesture by . . .
- A stranger offered me a random act of kindness by . . .

O GOD, WHO DOES NOT JUDGE WITH THE QUICKNESS OF THE HUMAN HEART, grace me with a wise and tender heart to grasp what others face in life; with a sure-footed willingness to walk in my brothers' and sisters' shoes and ease their pain; and with open hands to give generously to those in need without evaluation or suspicion. Rejoicing that you understand my own heart far more than I ever could and so do not judge me, may I return this favor to all those I meet. Amen.

> ❝ *Do not judge, so that you may not be judged. For with the judgment you make you will be judged, and the measure you give will be the measure you get.* ❞
> (Matt. 7:1–2)

20

Inventive Love
Compassion

FOR THIRTY-SEVEN YEARS, MISS VERNA ELLEN worked in the elementary school cafeteria. She was happiest serving breakfast so that she could get her "kiddies off to a smart and nutritious start." Enjoying children crunch their cereal, munch bananas, or slurp orange juice, she would make the rounds to check that homework was done, ask about siblings, and sometimes give words of comfort when the hamster was lost or the puppy was sick. Her presence was a daily vitamin boost.

A Story

Now retired from her cafeteria years and on a limited income, Miss Verna Ellen pledged inwardly to continue to feed the hungry. Unable to stand long hours, she realized that serving at her church's food pantry was impossible. So she decided to allot ten dollars a month for this worthy cause. But it is too easy, she thought, to simply put money in the Sunday collection plate. So, each month, Miss Verna Ellen goes food pantry shopping. She gets name brands because, as she shared, "the hungry probably eat enough generic. And just because people shop at a food bank doesn't mean *I* have to buy no-name sale items. After all, it's mighty nice to see *Cheerios* on a cereal box or *Skippy* on a peanut butter jar." Not everyone agrees with her philosophy, but no one questions her dedication.

There is the challenge of delivering her purchases to the pantry. No longer driving, Miss Verna Ellen takes a city bus to the closest stop near the food bank. Then, in all kinds of weather, she walks the half-mile, toting her goods. One day I asked, "Miss Verna Ellen, why don't you just bring the groceries to church and ask a pantry volunteer to deliver them for you? It would be so much easier and save you lots of time, don't you think?"

Miss Verna Ellen looked at me rather curiously, paused, and smiling said, "Love's got to be creative so it doesn't get drab or go cold. The bus ride and the long walk? All part of my gift."

Owning the Story, Opening to Grace

▪ I add the gift of time to serving others when I . . .

▪ I keep love and compassion warm and creative by . . .

▪ I seek the grace to remain faithful to . . .

O INNOVATIVE, COMPASSIONATE GOD, teach me creative ways of loving and carve these words upon my heart: "Love never gives up . . . Puts up with everything, Trusts God always, always looks for the best, Never looks back, but keeps going to the end. We don't yet see things clearly. We're squinting in a fog, peering through a mist. But it won't be long before the weather clears and the sun shines bright! We'll see it all then, see it all clearly as God sees us . . . But for right now, until that completeness, we have three things to do to lead us toward that consummation: Trust steadily in God, hope unswervingly, love extravagantly. And the best of the three is love" (1 Cor. 13:3–7, 12–13, THE MESSAGE).

"*Love is infinitely inventive.*"
(Vincent de Paul)

21

Jobs Well Done
Work

T WAS AN UNUSUAL REQUEST. "SISTER," JOE began, "I would like to ask a favor. Would you be willing to pass out money on the streets to those who are faithfully doing behind-the-scenes work or witnessing to goodness? I will supply the bills and the lapel pins but wish to remain anonymous. I'd like you to acknowledge a job well done and affirm a positive public attitude or a person's dignity. Or maybe you could just offer a word of thanks for a worker's tireless efforts."

A year later, fulfilling Joe's wish, I discovered that positive dispositions bring joy in public places, no task is too routine or insignificant to make a difference, and life abounds, in the hearts of people who give, if we take time to notice. I know because I met them.

There was seventy-four-year-old Nora, an efficient waitress in an airport restaurant, who, as she handed me my check, blessed me in God's name and then added that I look just like her older sister!

I met George, the steadfast vendor who stands under a Boston overpass intersection, in blizzard or blazing heat, selling newspapers to early morning commuters. "Business," he told me with an infectious laugh, "is always easier when the traffic light turns red."

Martha, the cleaning lady at a local Massachusetts bus station, scrubs toilets and sinks to a shine. "Most people never say a word to me so it's nice to be talked to," she commented after I admired the sparkling mirror.

I stood mesmerized as I watched Philip, the transit station's information booth attendant, energetically repeating the same city tourist directions. In a booming voice accentuated by a sense of adventure, he doubles as the arrivals and departures announcer.

Aaron is a café server in a chain bookstore. His job is to prepare cups of coffee and specialty teas according to customers' orders and satisfaction. He told me that it is his goal to go through life being an employee who takes time to do things well and carefully.

And then there is the nameless man with a magnetic personality who waves a sign on a downtown street corner. His sign says: "Got no change? Okay. I only want a smile. Go ahead and give one. It's free."

All of these people and so many more, in these unassuming tasks, are making the world a better place, filling it with service, beauty, care, and humor. As time went on, I realized that they *really* didn't need one of Joe's "Lend a Hand; Lift a Heart" lapel pins I had offered them along with a crisp twenty-dollar bill. Each in a special way was already making a contribution and boosting spirits.

Owning the Story, Opening to Grace

- ■ I tend to regard routine work as . . .
- ■ Someone who inspires me with a spirit of job dedication is . . .
- ■ A difficult task I perform well is . . .

GOD, you give many of us the privilege and opportunity to earn a daily wage. May our everyday labors join us more closely to others in dignity and service. May we be generous enough to share what we have with those who are unable to work. We ask that you bless us, help us realize that nothing is too insignificant to give you praise, and confirm us in the work we are asked to do. May this become our way of life. "Let the favor of the Lord our God be upon us, and prosper for us the work of our hands" (Ps 90:17).

❝ *God has created persons for all states in life, and in all of them we are inspired when we see people who fulfill their daily obligations with strength and dedication.* ❞

(Anthony Mary Claret)

22

Lego Castle
Heaven

SITTING ON THE FLOOR OF THE HIV/AIDS DAY CARE, five-year-old Bruce was playing in a pile of Legos. He was enjoying our after-school program as he waited for his father to pick him up. Pulling up a small chair to join him, I began to think about this child.

Articulate and gifted, he can skillfully build Lego trucks and robots, gets excited reading about hungry caterpillars and deep water sharks, and delights in dancing and sing-alongs, especially with his purple dinosaur television friend Barney. In fact, Bruce knows most of Barney's lines in these children's programs by heart.

Resilient and feisty, Bruce does not shy away from the challenges of his AIDS. He deals with his tube feedings as well as wearing his orange and blue backpack containing his medicinal infusions, vital to his survival. This pack may hamper his playground adventures but never dampens his spirits.

Bruce bears not only the medical demands of his disease but also the emotional weight of parental separation anxiety due to his mother's death. In spite of his own pain and child's grief, he reaches out to all his friends with sensitivity beyond his years and a comfort beyond his own illness.

His humming, as he built with the Legos, brought me back from my reverie.

"What are you making, Bruce?" I asked. I saw a red wall with a wide opening in the center. And curious as teachers can be, I wondered what his creativity was constructing.

"I'm building a part of heaven," Bruce placidly replied. "When you die, you go to God's beautiful castle. The door is always open, but you got to walk in with Jesus."

"You're so right," I gulped, swallowing the lump in my throat.

I could only surmise that Bruce suspected, and perhaps often thought about, what we adults knew with certainty. His weakened body was rapidly succumbing to AIDS, and Jesus, holding his hand, would soon lead him through heaven's door, bringing him home.

Owning the Story, Opening to Grace

- My vision of heaven is . . .
- I would like my dying words to be . . .
- I remember the last words of my . . .

ETERNAL WORD, thank you for the dying words of children and of holy women and men that fill our hearts with hope for heaven. Grant that my final words may echo my love for you and bring others consolation and peace. May my heart sing now and at the hour of my death: "Precious Lord, take my hand.

Lead me on. Let me stand. Through the storm, through the night, lead me on to light. Take my hand, precious Lord, and lead me home" (African American spiritual).

"If you love me, do not weep. If you only knew the gift of God and what heaven is! If only you could hear the angels' songs from where you are, and see me among them! If you could only see before your eyes the eternal fields with their horizons and the new paths in which I walk! If only you could contemplate for one moment the Beauty that I see."

(Augustine of Hippo, written of his mother Monica)

23

Life on the Subway
Divine Reflections

O N A LONG RIDE ON THE "T," THE POPULAR NAME for the Boston transit system, I began to people watch. What sparked this interest was a man tap dancing in front of the glass exit doors. Humming along with his iPod and oblivious to everything, he clicked and clacked with rhythm and precision. His grin signaled that he was pleased with his impromptu routine.

A Story

In the end seat next to the dancer, a young girl sported a T-shirt proclaiming "Time to be Disruptive." However, she sat calmly, straining her neck as she turned backwards to check the name of every station along the way. At each stop, she took out a small mirror from her backpack, examined her lips, applied more flamingo-hued lipstick, smacked, smiled, and returned to her thoughts. I wondered if she was trying to use up an outdated color or going to meet a very important person.

Farther down the row of plastic seats was a middle-aged woman wearing earrings hanging from her ear lobes to her shoulders. The glitzy, three-inch adornments matched both her showy orange and yellow necklace and her glitter-enhanced gel fingernails. She exuded a sense of feeling gorgeous with her appearance.

The relatively quiet atmosphere in the subway car was interrupted by a man diligently planning, via his cell phone, another carpet delivery. He kept insisting that he *did* have the right date but was not given the correct time. So it was not his fault that he had to reschedule. He was adamant that he would not give a discount for failure to show up or reimburse the customer for her office time lost. I was curious as to who would win!

Next to the rug installer sat a bearded gentleman with a toothless smile playing peek-a-boo with a baby in a stroller. He may have been a distraction for his neighbor studying *How to Speak English in Ten Days.* Given that *this* gentleman appeared to be in his eighties, I chuckled that ten days may not be enough.

Quietly sitting next to the earnest language student was a teenager reading a letter, playing a game on her iPad, and bopping her head in time with the music streaming from her iPod. *At what age does multitasking yield to doing one thing at a time?* I daydreamed.

Life was alive and well on this subway car. But, beyond my personal feelings of vitality and connectedness, these people spoke to me of God. We have a God who can dance with us in the rhythms of our life, accepts our superficial attempts at glamour and relishes our inner beauty, and tolerates all our excuses and gives us the benefit of the doubt. This God of ours enjoys our games of peek-a-boo with the divine presence in our daily routine, speaks our language and understands our faltering words, and patiently waits for us to let go of the rush and noise of life so as to discover the hush and silence of prayer.

"Quincy Center Station," announced the mechanical computer voice. It was my stop. Glancing one more time at the passengers, I made my way to the exit door, convinced that each of us, even as we ride the subway, speaks of God to one another.

Owning the Story, Opening to Grace

■ I feel a connection with others when I . . .

■ People watching teaches me that God . . .

■ God guides me by . . .

O GOD OF MY JOURNEY, may I always seek you in the highways and byways of life. May you speak to me through strangers in the parking lot, on the subway, or in a plane. May I reverence you in all these people, in all events, and in all circumstances. Grant me the grace to find you everywhere and, rejoicing in the discovery, know that you clear my path, travel with me, and guide me in the way of everlasting life.

" Be in all things a God seeker and at all times a God finder, among all kinds of people and in all kinds of circumstances. "

(Meister Eckhart)

24

Light from Above
Wisdom

WHAT PRECISELY IS THE GIFT OF WISDOM? It is not easy to bundle up this gift of the Holy Spirit. In an effort to explain its meaning, my tendency is to speak far too long with too many words. They always seemed to miss the mark, like a shot in the dark, until I heard a New Jersey parish priest's streamlined comparison:

A Story

"The difference between being smart and being wise is like the difference between a light bulb and a star in the sky. The light bulb has a switch but the star has God."

Wisdom is a gift of the heart, centered on experience, not a collection of concepts learned through books or years of study. It is the beam of light that permeates everything and reveals to us the presence of God in each person, event, and circumstance in life. It is the glow of gentleness in the midst of a harsh world; the glimmer of hope that shines across the dark sky of suffering and pain; the shafts of comfort that come when our life is in disarray. This gift is the radiance that shines through acts of loving forgiveness as we live with the mind of Christ, and the glare of self-knowledge that calls us to personal transformation.

Wisdom is the north star of our journey that shows us the path to walk and lets us know where we are headed. It is the illumination of experiencing within our being, and not merely in our heads, that "no eye has seen, nor ear heard, nor the human heart conceived, what God has prepared for those who love him" (1 Cor. 2:9). As we anticipate the refulgence of what is yet to come, can we be wise and stand in awe under the night sky and bask in the glow of the twinkling stars?

Owning the Story, Opening to Grace

■ One experience that deepened wisdom within me is . . .

■ For me the Holy Spirit's gift of wisdom can be compared to . . .

■ I can bring someone a glimmer of hope and a shaft of comfort by . . .

O GOD OF WISDOM, place your Spirit within that I may "show by my good life that my works are done with gentleness born of wisdom. The wisdom from above is first pure, then peaceable, gentle, willing to yield, full of mercy and good fruits, without a trace of partiality or hypocrisy" (adapted from Jas. 3:13, 17). "Reveal this wisdom, secret and hidden, which you decreed before the ages for our glory. Speak to me of things taught by the Spirit until I have the mind of Christ" (adapted from 1 Cor. 2:7, 13, 16). Amen.

> *Wisdom is radiant and unfading,*
> *and she is easily discerned*
> *by those who love her,*
> *and is found by those who seek her.*
> *She hastens to make herself known to those who desire her.*
> *One who rises early to seek her*
> *will have no difficulty,*
> *for she will be found sitting at the gate.*

(Wisd. 6:12–14)

25

My Left Hand
Almsgiving

ENT WAS AROUND THE CORNER. MY FIFTH graders, in the grip of frigid temperatures, indoor recesses, and winter restlessness, were distracted, uninterested, and unmotivated. It would be a challenge to prepare them for the upcoming liturgical season as well as to inspire them to give generously to the Catholic Relief Services' annual school drive.

Today's religion class just happened to be about Jesus's teaching on almsgiving (Matt. 6:3–4). As a teacher, I began priming my students for generous sacrifice: giving in secret without counting the cost; donating from their allowance and not from a parent's pocket; and contributing unselfishly for the good of the world.

Suddenly, I noticed Gregory Paul twisting, turning, flinging out his right hand, and simultaneously shaking his left hand over his head and behind his back. Thinking that he was not paying attention or seeking attention with all these monkeyshines, I inquired with a gentle but firm voice, coupled with my teacher's look, "Gregory Paul, what *are* you doing?"

"Sister," he replied, "I am practicing. I know you said that Jesus said when you do nice things your left hand shouldn't know what your right hand is doing. Did Jesus know how hard that is? When my right hand puts money in the poor box, my left hand doesn't know where to go."

Jesus makes it clear that *how* we give is just as important as *what* we give. Almsgiving is a spontaneous response to a need at hand. It happens quietly, with no thought of how this contribution or assistance will benefit me, win personal applause, or polish my reputation in my neighborhood community or parish. Giving without being noticed is to follow the way of Christ. Our secret acts of charity and sharing strip away our pride, purify our intentions, and transform a handout into a gospel witness.

Owning the Story, Opening to Grace

▪ Almsgiving in secret purifies my intentions by . . .

▪ I add the sacrifice of time to the treasure of giving when . . .

▪ My attitude toward supporting global charities is . . .

O GOD OF MY ALMSGIVING, bestow your strength and courage upon me as I try to:

Value the quality of my giving.

Openhandedly contribute from my need and then add a bit extra.

Let acts of charity be between you and me.

Hand over for the good of others what I would like to keep for myself.

Lavishly give without trying to shine my reputation.

I bring these desires to your heart and pray in the name of Jesus.

Amen.

“ *But when you give alms, do not let your left hand know what your right hand is doing, so that your alms may be done in secret; and your Father who sees in secret will reward you.* ”

(Matt. 6:3–4)

26

Never Done Before
Death

WITH BOUNDLESS ENERGY AND RELENTLESS in pursuing justice for all, Ursuline Sister Mary Jude Jun lived a life of total giving: many long years of dedicated friendship to a prisoner on death row; tireless efforts for equal rights and empowerment of women, especially African Americans; and personal commitments to myriad social issues from Appalachian coal mining mountain destruction to the ravages of global hunger. She was unafraid to speak out, walk picket lines, or boycott stores for unfair labor practices.

▪ A Story

But, she confided, she lived with a personal fear: that one day she would wake up and be told she had cancer. She had witnessed many of her friends cope with the physical challenges of chemotherapy and radiation treatments. This anxiety overshadowed her even in her bravest moments.

One day, Sister Mary Jude felt lethargic, dizzy, and unwell. A week later medical tests confirmed the one thing she most dreaded: terminal cancer.

As she lay dying, calmly and in trust, visitors streamed to say farewell. Sister Mary Jude asked each one about personal concerns that, over time, she had made her own. As the days passed, she began to grow weary but managed to muster enough strength for the constant goodbyes and her personal funeral preparations.

"How are you doing?" asked one of the pastoral care staff, quietly and with great concern.

"I *really* don't know," Sister Mary Jude responded with a weakened voice and a smile. "I've never died before."

Would that we could take lessons in what to expect and how it feels to die or what it is like to see the face of the God we have tried to love for a lifetime. But death will always be God's best-kept secret and remains our test. Dying is like those first steps we took as a child after our mother let go and our father extended waiting arms, or that game of blindfolded trust walks we enjoyed in summer camp, or perhaps even the times we were encouraged to fall backward into another's outstretched arms.

In each instance all we could do was trust the one who promised to reach for us, guide us, or catch us.

At the moment of our death, we trust that God will grasp us in our hesitant steps of surrender, will lead us by the hand through the dark valley, and will embrace us as we fall into the divine arms. True, we have never died before, but certainly the moment of our death will confirm what we have known all through our life: God is always with us.

Owning the Story, Opening to Grace

▪ One lesson I learned from the death of a loved one is . . .

▪ What I fear most about death is . . .

▪ In thinking of my own death, I ask for the grace this week to . . .

O GOD OF EVERLASTING LIFE, grant eternal rest to:

All our deceased family members and friends.

All who died alone with no one to pray for them.

All who died in great pain and suffering.

Victims of war, starvation, neglect, and addiction.

Children around the world who have died in refugee camps and on city streets.

All who have died in accidents, natural disasters, and by suicide.

And to all those who feel they are dying by depression, hopelessness, or grief, grant your peace.

We pray this in the name of your resurrected Son and our Brother, Jesus Christ. Amen.

"*But the souls of the righteous are in the hand of God,*
and no torment will ever touch them.
In the eyes of the foolish they seemed to have died,
and their departure was thought to be a disaster,
and their going from us to be their destruction;
but they are at peace.
The faithful will abide with him in love,
because grace and mercy are upon his only ones,
and he watches over his elect."

(Wisdom 3:1–3, 9)

27

Night in the Forest
Trust

I T WAS A DIFFICULT TIME FOR THE SMALL PARISH. There was an unconfirmed rumor circulating that it was on the verge of being closed. Attendance was down, morale was low, and bills were mounting. The pastor, Father Eugene, knowing of the growing negative sentiments, told a story from the Native American tradition about protection and trust.

A Story

There was a boy who, according to the tribal custom, was brought to the forest in his thirteenth year. To measure his courage and to evaluate if he was ready to be accepted as an adult into the tribe, he was left alone. Before long, the forest was encased in darkness without even a sliver of moonlight.

The lad became afraid. Every swaying of the trees, every night noise from the leaves and bushes, terrified him. Imagining the worst, he was certain the forest was fraught with danger and evil. Unable to quell his fears and realizing that there was no way out in the blackness, the boy was unable to sleep.

For the entire night the youth sat hunched over near some undergrowth, cupping his hands around his ears, trying to block out the pounding of his racing heart and the sound of his heavy breathing. He was more scared than he had ever been in his life.

The light of dawn finally brought the budding adolescent relief. Looking around, he was surprised to see a shadowy figure nearby. *It looks like my father*, he thought. Sure enough, from behind a tree came his father, arms outstretched. The boy realized that his father had been watching him all night long, standing guard to protect him from harm, and ready, at a moment's notice, to save him from danger.

The boy beamed at his father, joyfully exclaiming, "Father, if I had known you were watching over me, I would have slept the whole night through."

Like Father Eugene's parish, we all have situations that stretch our faith, whether it be sagging morale, mounting financial concerns, or major life questions and worries. They can clump together like a forest, blocking our view or creating haunting images that disturb our peace. Sometimes like the Native American boy, we want to flee, but there seems to be no way out; other times, we simply sit immobilized by fear or dread. It may take a dark night of faith, but if we persevere, light is as certain as the dawn. And God, who has stood behind every tree, will come out of hiding, thank us for our endurance, and embrace us in parental love. In that moment we realize that, throughout it all, God was with us. And we can make up for lost sleep.

Owning the Story, Opening to Grace

- I lend a hand to those in difficult times by . . .
- To persevere through a crisis I . . .
- God protected me on one occasion when . . .

GOD WHO WATCHES OVER ME, may "I bind unto myself today your power to hold and to lead; your eye to watch; your might to stay; your ear to hearken to my need.

"May I bind unto myself today your wisdom, my God, to teach; your hand to guide; your shield to ward; your word, my God, to give me speech; and your heavenly host to be my guard." Amen.
(Attributed to Patrick of Ireland)

❝ *God is not a deceiver that he should offer to support us and be with us, and then, when we lean upon him or need him, should slip away from us.* ❞

(Augustine of Hippo)

28

Ocean Thoughts
Poverty

REMEMBER IT WELL. IT WAS A CLOUDLESS May afternoon, and I was nestled in the curve of a rock on the jagged Maine coastline. We had an hour's break before the next session of the "Attitudes and Approaches to Poverty" conference that I was attending. So far, it had been worthwhile, but there were many erudite notions and analyses going around. Having brought my journal with me, I decided to spend this time letting the wise reflections of my students surge from its pages and crash upon my heart just as the waves were pounding the boulders.

"My daddy and I were talking about the poor. He said that the bottom line is that we help the poor. Then I asked Daddy if the top line is that we love them" (Reese, age nine).

▪ A Story

"Once I saw a poor person lying on the street. My dad said he hoped he would get on his feet. But I don't think he meant just stand up" (Jack, age nine).

"Poor people are some of the greatest people alive. I mean they work every single day to survive and that takes courage" (Brady, age ten).

"What really makes a person poor? When you got ripped clothes or when you ruin your life?" (Guy, age ten).

"I never saw a poor person, but I keep asking God to let me meet one, 'cause I always keep a treat in my pocket for them" (Lowell, age eight).

"People are rich when they go after what they need, but they are real poor when they just keep a-wantin' more" (Della May, age ten).

"My neighbor thinks that hungry people who steal should be put in jail. But I think just thinking that is a crime" (Barrett, age eleven).

"I had lots of money in my piggy bank. My big brother broke it and threw my pennies all over the house. Now I have to look for them every day after school. Because even my last penny belongs to the poor" (Michelle, age seven).

The children have it right, I thought, as the roundup call came to return to the workshop.

Eleven years ago I closed my journal. These children are now approaching young adulthood; I am in another decade of life. But the truths they spoke remain as solid and enduring as the rock upon which I sat.

When we add love to material assistance, we help others get on their feet. When we admire the courage of daily survival, we suppress judgments of the needy. When we know our wants from our needs, we give all we can and even a bit extra.

Jesus reminds us that we will "always have the poor with [us]" (Matt. 26:11). But my student Mercy has a hope: "Even though we can't make it so that nobody is poor, at least we can help make it the best for them." If this ten-year-old's approach to poverty would become the attitude of our heart, just imagine the change in our world!

Owning the Story, Opening to Grace

■ I would describe my attitude and approach toward the poor as . . .

■ A time I gave from my need with a touch of love was . . .

■ A judgment of the poor that I feel called to change is . . .

GOD OF THE POOR, grant me "the strength to rescue the homeless when they cry out; to help those who are poor and in need; to extend kindness to the weak and the helpless; and to protect the children and infirm" (adapted from Ps. 72:12–14). May I realize that "you chose me to bring justice; that you sent me to bring light and hope; and that you will always be at my side as I try to fulfill your command" (adapted from Isa. 42:6).

> *Commitment to the poor is based on the Gospel of Jesus Christ: it does not have to rely on a political manifesto.*
>
> (Pope John Paul II)

29

Out of Nowhere
Protection

ONLY MINUTES BEFORE, THE SKY DANCED IN A soft spring blue. Now dark clouds hung ominously in the sky, signaling an imminent torrential downpour. *Get going to the convent*, I commanded myself, *or you will really get caught in a bad storm.*

No sooner had I started the engine and begun my return trip than the heavens burst open and large hail began to fall, pounding the white Oldsmobile with a fury. Realizing I was right near a church, I pulled into the parking lot and nervously slipped my rosary from my pocket. My heart was pounding in my chest. "Fear is useless; what is needed is trust," I repeated between the Hail Marys.

After what seemed like hours, the quarter-sized hail ceased

and the rain tapered off. Renewing my courage, I decided to inch my way home. I did not get very far when I noticed that the street I always took was flooded. Following the detouring vehicles, I ended up lost on an unfamiliar side road. I had no idea where I was and unwisely convinced myself that the car could make it through the deep puddle I saw in front of me. I was wrong and, after sputtering and coughing, the car stalled. Fear inundated me. "God, send help!" I called out in panic, not really believing that anyone could hear me or would even come to my aid. Sinking into the driver's seat, I waited, brooded, and scolded myself for being foolish.

A very short time later, a man approached my open passenger window. "I'm stuck," I moaned.

"I know," the kind voice said. "And I am a mechanic and have just what you need to dry out the engine. You'll be fine."

"A mechanic? I can't believe it." I laughed in joyful relief.

The unknown stranger lifted the hood and began to blow canned compressed air into the engine. When the container was empty, he said, "Now start the car."

Sure enough, the twelve-year-old automobile sprang into life with a soft purr as though nothing had happened.

"Sir," I said, "I don't know how you knew I was here. I don't know how to thank you. I don't even *know* your name." Then I whimsically added, "Guess I will just have to call you 'Angel.'"

"That will do," he replied, stretching out his hand, half in blessing, half to say goodbye.

I attached my seat belt and turned to the window to offer a grateful handshake. But the mechanic was gone, nowhere in sight. And on the passenger seat lay the empty can.

Owning the Story, Opening to Grace

■ An angel once came to my help when . . .

■ I can trust the protection of God when . . .

■ In trust and confidence, I will be an angel for another this week by . . .

O GOD WHO PROTECTS ME, may I believe that, in your care, you have sent your divine messengers to watch over us. May they be ever at my side "to light and guard, rule and guide." May these words of Scripture take root in my heart and increase my faith:

"I am going to send an angel in front of you, to guard you on the way and to bring you to the place that I have prepared. Be attentive to him and listen to his voice" (Exod. 23:20–21).

"This poor soul cried, and was heard by the LORD, and was saved from every trouble.

The angel of the LORD encamps

around those who fear him, and delivers them" (Ps. 34:6–7).

"The angel said to her, 'Do not be afraid'" (Luke 1:30).

"Then I looked, and I heard the voice of many angels surrounding the throne . . . singing with full voice,

'Worthy is the Lamb . . .

to receive . . . honor and glory and blessing'"

(Rev. 5:11–12).

"*By an angel I mean any person or event that has changed
the whole course of our life, influenced our behavior, helped
us in need, made us turn right when we were about to turn
left, and in general made us better. Such a concept is sooner
or later seen as being an act of God.*"

(Fulton J. Sheen)

30

Piece of Cake
Fasting

WAS SEVENTEEN YEARS OLD AND SIX MONTHS
in the convent when Lent rolled around. Our Lenten
practices were very strict, with religious formation traditions
added to the Church requirements. Since it was my first time
experiencing these rigors, I struggled to put aside thoughts of
what I had previously enjoyed: crunchy potato chips, cold soda,
spearmint gum, and gooey chocolate bars. Our meals were
meager with no snacks in between.

A Story

This particular day I was dealing with a stifling headache that seemed like a pressure cap squeezing every vein. And I was just plain hungry. Although we were encouraged to bear such inconveniences without speaking about them, I decided to confide in a beloved elderly nun who had been in the convent for sixty years. I was confident she would understand my difficult situation and perhaps even reveal her time-tested secret to coping. Seeing her in the hall, I hastened over and guiltily whispered, "Sister Emmanuel, can you help me out? Lent and fasting are really getting to me. I have a splitting headache."

With a crooked smile and gentle eyes that challenged yet soothed me, Sister Emmanuel summed up an aspect of this religious tradition. "What, my dear sister, did you expect? Fasting is no piece of cake."

Indeed, fasting is a challenge. Our stomachs rumble and thoughts wander to crispy carrots, savory salsa omelets, and gourmet desserts. We may even plan the menu for our next dinner party or muse about which restaurant we will patronize on a night out. In a word, we get a good taste of what it is like to be hungry.

But there is more to fasting than just foregoing dessert, skipping a meal, or drinking liquids for a day. True fasting calls us to even tougher spiritual practices. It asks us to give up griping about small inconveniences and become grateful for everyday life, refrain from harsh judgments and give others the benefit of the doubt, and replace anxious worry with confidence in divine providence.

When we open the sacred door of fasting, whether from food or critical attitudes, we discover that we are nourished, fed, and sustained in our spiritual life.

Owning the Story, Opening to Grace

▪ One way I can program fasting into my life is . . .

▪ God calls me to fast from the negative attitude of . . .

▪ I can replace anxious worry with a feast of trust by . . .

O GOD OF MY FASTING, may I:

Fast from judging others and feast on Christ indwelling in them.

Fast from discontent and feast on gratitude.

Fast from anger and feast on patience.

Fast from pessimism and feast on optimism.

Fast from bitterness and feast on forgiveness.

Fast from discouragement and feast on hope.

Fast from complaining and feast on appreciation.

Fast from worry and feast on trust.

Fast from false appearances and feast on inner beauty.

Fast from thoughts that weaken and feast on promises that inspire.

I ask this in your Holy Name, O good and gracious God, Amen.

(from a traditional Lenten prayer, origin unknown)

Is not this the fast that I choose:
to loose the bonds of injustice,
to undo the thongs of the yoke,
to let the oppressed go free,
and to break every yoke?
Is it not to share your bread with the hungry,
and bring the homeless poor into your house;
when you see the naked, to cover them,
and not hide yourself from your own kin?

(Isa. 58:6–7)

31

Prison Grace
Redemption

'VE ONLY GOT NINE TO NINETEEN YEARS LEFT," Melinda whispered in a hopeful voice. "But counting only makes matters worse, I guess." She and I had become friends during my year as a volunteer at the maximum-security facility. Now it was time to say goodbye as I was leaving for the desert of Sudan to feed children of the famine.

I only knew bits and pieces of Melinda's story, learned slowly over time. She was doing time, fifteen to twenty-five years, for

A Story

selling drugs on the streets of New York. But she did not want a prison sentence to stunt her personal growth. She was trying, on a daily basis, to make the most of her situation: taking reading and computer courses, learning household management skills, and attending personality development classes to increase her self-esteem. Most of all, she was proud to have been chosen to direct the arts and crafts program in the small center for children who were visiting their incarcerated mothers.

"I had so many hopes for my own children," Melinda mused. "But hopes need money. I mean, you just get tired living in a one-room apartment, coping with bills from one meager paycheck to another, and always afraid of neighborhood violence and gangs. Somebody told me that selling drugs paves the streets with gold, and I believed it. Made poor choices for good reasons, and now I'm paying hard. What hurts the most is that it's been three years since I've seen my own children." Her mother's love was staring through the bars of her inmate's heart.

Then Melinda, quietly reflecting, said, "I know God forgives me, but it's not easy for me to forgive myself. I decided to love other people's children to make up for what I've done. I sure would feed those starving children in Sudan, if I could, so you feed them in my name."

Melinda paused painfully. Leaving her inner cell and coming back to reality, she delightedly said, "Enough on that. I've got a surprise for you. I've been working on it little by little when you weren't here."

She went over to an opened cupboard, stretched her hands to the top shelf, and reached for a package protected in brown crinkled paper. Carefully unwrapping it, she said, "I bet you'll miss flowers in the desert as much as I do here in prison. When that happens, think about these." Then, with care and concern, Melinda lovingly placed a bouquet of handmade yellow paper roses into my arms. In that thoughtful gesture, two lives were intertwined with grace: one with healing for what lay behind; the other, with courage for what lay ahead in a barren African desert.

Owning the Story, Opening to Grace

- ▪ I made a poor choice for a good reason when I . . .
- ▪ With God's grace I can break the chains of . . .
- ▪ I will sacrifice for someone in prison by . . .

O GIVER OF REDEEMING GRACE, in your mercy, encourage
  and comfort:
Political prisoners who live without hope.
Those serving time for making poor choices for good reasons.
Those jailed through false accusations or insufficient evidence.
Incarcerated men and women who are trying to rebuild their
  lives.
Inmates who are mistreated, judged, and scorned.

Those on death row who struggle with despair and searing guilt. I pray this in the name of Jesus, your beloved Son and our forgiving Redeemer. Amen.

> ❝ *Let us therefore approach the throne of grace with bold-ness, so that we may receive mercy and find grace to help in time of need.* ❞
>
> (Heb. 4:16)

32

Putting on a Show
Praise

I N EARLY SEPTEMBER I INTRODUCED MY FIFTH graders to journaling. Sometimes my students sat stone-faced for the ten minutes, and other times I could hear their pencils scratching across their notebook paper. Initially all entries were both personal and confidential. By springtime, they asked to have regular opportunities to share with the class what they had written.

One April morning Frank, his hand waving wildly in the air, volunteered to read his journal entry from the previous day. I took a deep professorial breath, the kind teachers take when they have no idea what's coming.

■ A Story

"Well," he began, impishly grinning, "here's what I wrote: Today was some day at school. All of a sudden, the wind blew up, it got dark, and hail balls fell. The windows rattled and, boy, was there loud thunder. Even the lights went out. Sister told us to stay in our desks, fold our hands, and don't dare move. But I think God wanted us to run to the window and enjoy the show he was putting on."

Frank was right. God puts on so many shows: the swath of the Milky Way across the desert sky of Sudan, a shooting star on an October night in New Hampshire, flashes of lightning illuminating a dark Appalachian hollow, vast galaxies that hide behind the twinkling winter planets, pounding rain and peals of thunder that douse summer's heavy air, and falling snow that quiets Mother Earth and her children in Maine.

It took a child to get me out of my desk, unfold my hands, and run to the window. Now, when God choreographs such events, I think of Frank as I jump to my feet, burst forth in "wow," and with a standing ovation praise God for superb performances.

Owning the Story, Opening to Grace

■ When I stand under the stars, I sometimes feel . . .

■ The beauties of creation that move me to wonder and awe are . . .

■ The next time I feel the wind in my face or hear the rain, I will ask for the grace to . . .

"MOST HIGH, ALMIGHTY, GOOD LORD,
All praise, glory, honor, and exaltation are yours!
To you alone do they belong,
And no mere mortal dares pronounce your name.
Praised be you, my Lord, through Sister Moon and the stars,
In the heavens you have made them clear, precious, and
　　beautiful.
Praised be you, my Lord, through Brother Wind,
And fair and stormy seasons
and all heaven's varied moods,
by which you nourish all that you have made.
Praised be you through our Sister Water,
so useful, lowly, precious, and pure.
All creatures
Praise and glorify you, my Lord,
And give you thanks
And serve you in great humility." (Canticle of Creation, Francis
　　of Assisi)

> *The heavens are telling the glory of God;*
> *And the firmament proclaims his handiwork.*
> (Ps. 19:1)

33

Quilting Squares
Gospel Living

IT WAS A COWORKER REFLECTION DAY AT URSULINE Academy in Kirkwood, Missouri. Terri Folsom Rogan, the director of mission effectiveness, was our speaker for a mini retreat.

"Preach the gospel at all times; when necessary, use words," she began. "This is one of my favorite quotes, attributed to St. Francis of Assisi, and it is how I saw my grandmother live."

Terri's grandmother, Mourna Hester, quit school in sixth grade to help her parents raise her seven younger siblings. She learned to sew and made the clothes they needed; tended a garden and canned vegetables; and, as a young woman, lovingly and devotedly held her dying mother in her arms.

"Just as she was present to everyone in her family as she grew up, so was she there for each one of her grandchildren as she aged. Without words, she fulfilled the gospel call to care for others," Terri continued.

When she was seventy-five, Mourna rode roller coasters with Terri. At seventy-eight, she joined Terri sleigh riding down a steep hill and making backyard Christmas Eve snow angels. In her presence and in her laughter, Terri experienced the gospel exhortation to find joy in everyday experiences and nature's surprises.

When Mourna was eighty-eight, dementia knocked at her door, slowly making its way inside. It was now Terri's turn to care for her. Knowing Mourna feared taking a bath, Terri decided one day to turn the bathroom into a spa environment with candles, music, and bubble bath. Mourna watched with childlike eyes, and Terri told us that, as she bathed her grandmother from head to toe, she experienced God's presence as never before. It was a spiritual watershed moment as her grandmother, in her mental confusion and physical vulnerability, witnessed to the gospel challenge of surrender.

Shortly after Terri moved Mourna into an assisted living facility, they were spending time together one day. In the middle of their visit, Mourna opened one of her drawers and pulled out her quilting squares to show her granddaughter. Mourna had lost the ability to cut the material evenly, and her stitches were far bigger than she would have ever allowed in her "glory days" of quilting. But she was no less proud of her accomplishments. Terri ran her fingers over each square with admiration and respect. Mourna, smiling broadly, carefully put them back in the drawer.

Two minutes later, Mourna again removed the squares from their place in her dresser and proudly displayed her efforts as though she and Terri were having this conversation for the first time. Terri's admiration was repeated; her grandmother's satisfaction obvious, she once again returned her squares to their special spot. This "in and out the drawer" ritual went on for the better part of an hour.

"In that visit with her," Terri concluded, "my grandmother taught me that every single moment is fresh and filled with wonder. She assured me that we can always begin again, moment after moment; that we can believe that all things are ever made new; that we are to see all things, all people, as though for the first time. On that February day, my beloved grandmother, without words, once again preached the gospel with her life and from a drawer filled with quilting squares."

Owning the Story, Opening to Grace

■ Someone who preaches the gospel without words is . . .
■ A time I listened to a repetitive story as though for the first time was . . .
■ I can witness to the gospel call to begin again when . . .

O GOOD NEWS GOD, may I proclaim your holy gospel: by compassionately caring for others in my daily routines; by enjoying everyday events and unexpected fun times; by confidently surrendering to situations beyond my control; and, most of all, by rejoicing in the knowledge that each moment holds a fresh start, a new beginning. May your gospel take root in my heart, and may I proclaim it in all the ways I live. Amen.

"*And they went out and proclaimed the good news every-where, while the Lord worked with them and confirmed the message by the signs that accompanied it.*"
(Mk. 16:20)

34

Red Sky
Love

PLOPPING INTO A SEAT ON THE BOSTON TRAIN and leaning back to relax, I began recalling the refreshing weekend I had spent in New Hampshire with my mother and my sister Courtney. We went out for lunch but, other than that, just sat around enjoying each other's company. As we did so, I looked into my mama's eyes, sacred doors to the store of God's love that she poured out into the lives of her family, friends, and neighbors.

In the midst of my thoughts about this special family visit, I glanced out the window, only to discover fire-engine-red splashes of color masterfully thrown across the dusking sky. I was not the only one to notice, as the gentleman in front of me turned around and excitedly encouraged, "Miss, catch the sky. I have never seen anything like it."

"Neither have I," I replied. "It's magnificent, sir, and just takes my breath away." I felt as though I were watching something that would never happen again as the brilliant red gradually faded into a soft pink afterglow, and then it was night.

As soon as I got home, I dashed to the phone. "Mama," I said, gasping as she answered, "I saw the most spectacular sunset while I was on the train." I recounted my experience, adding that, if I had not seen it myself, I would never have believed the sky could be so blazing, so intense.

There was a short pause and then Mama sweetly replied with undeniable conviction, "Sugar, I know God sent that red sky just for you. It was his special valentine." I had forgotten it was February 14.

Owning the Story, Opening to Grace

- God makes me feel special when . . .
- I make others feel special when . . .
- This week I promise to notice messages of divine love by . . .

COVENANT GOD, do not let me miss any of the many ways you have of showing your faithful love for me. Grant me the grace to wholeheartedly live by these reminders:

"O my strength, I will sing praises to you,
for you, O God, are my fortress,
the God who shows me steadfast love." (Ps. 59:17)

"It is good to give thanks to the LORD,
to sing praises to your name, O Most High;
to declare your steadfast love in the morning,
and your faithfulness by night." (Ps. 92:1–2)

"I have loved you with an everlasting love;
therefore I have continued my faithfulness to you." (Jer. 31:3)

"As the Father has loved me, so I have loved you;
abide in my love." (John 15:9)

"In all these things we are more than conquerors through him
who loved us. For I am convinced that neither death, nor life,
nor angels, nor rulers, nor things present, nor things to come,
nor powers, nor height, nor depth, nor anything else in all
creation, will be able to separate us from the love of God in
Christ Jesus our Lord." (Rom. 8:37–39)

"In this is love, not that we loved God but that he loved us."
(1 Jn. 4:10)

❝ *God made the universe transparent, like a windowpane.
Everything created tells something about God's love, for 'by
the visible things of the world is the Invisible God made
manifest' (Rom. 1:20).* ❞

(Fulton J. Sheen)

35

Rich Young Man and a Teddy Bear
Discipleship

EIGHT-YEAR-OLD MILLICENT WAS THE "GIVE-away" queen of my second grade. Every few weeks she would share with me what video game, Barbie doll, or Crayola collection she had chosen to put in her decorated box destined for those in need. But she never mentioned Bo, her favorite teddy bear, whose orange velvet vest sported bows of all colors and sizes. I'd notice her chubby face peeking up over Millicent's backpack and, every once in a while, with varied nods and smiles she would stuff Bo in her desk. Millicent had a very special relationship with her teddy bear.

One day, Millicent came half walking, half dragging, into my learning center. The expression on her face reflected a blend of contentment and a struggling sadness. I realized something was awry when her tightly zipped backpack did not have a furry nose poking out. "Well," she began, "I thought it was time for Bo to make someone else happy like me. So I was hugging her when Mommy told me it was time to put her in my pretty box for the poor. But sometimes you need a few extra minutes with something you love."

We can be enslaved like the rich young man in Mark's Gospel (Mk. 10:17–22) or generous like Millicent in my second grade. There are many things that hold our hearts captive: our status symbols and financial success; power and prized personal fame; unyielding self-righteous opinions and judgments. Whatever our possessions or selfish behaviors, Jesus looks at us with the same tender love he had for the rich young man and for Millicent. He offers us the same challenging invitation: to let go of all that fetters us and share what we love with the needy, whether it be a valuable possession or a cuddly teddy bear. Then, with expectant hope, Jesus waits to see which way we will go, even if it takes a little time for us to say goodbye.

Owning the Story, Opening to Grace

▪ The possessions, status symbols, and behaviors that enslave me are . . .
▪ To follow Christ more closely, I would like to . . .
▪ One of my heart's treasures is . . .

JESUS OF LOVING YET CHALLENGING INVITATIONS, teach me to live your words: "Do not store up for yourselves treasures on earth, where moth and rust consume and where thieves break in and steal; but store up for yourselves treasures in heaven, where neither moth nor rust consumes and where thieves do not break in and steal. For where your treasure is, there your heart will be also" (Matt. 6:19–21).

> ❝ *Jesus, looking at him, loved him and said, 'You lack one thing; go, sell what you own, and give the money to the poor, and you will have treasure in heaven; then come, follow me.' When he heard this, he was shocked and went away grieving, for he had many possessions.* ❞
>
> (Mk. 10:21–22)

36

Ruffles and Ribbons
Holiness

WITH A SPRING IN HER STEP, A CAPTIVATING smile on her face, holding her grandmother's hand, the six-year-old bounded into the parish church before Sunday Mass. She had obviously chosen her outfit herself: pink striped shoes, an orange dress with ruffles that hung below her knees, and a green and blue flowered scarf tied loosely around her neck. Completing her ensemble was a headful of pink and orange ribbons, a cloth sunflower purse, and a child's satisfaction in her appearance.

As they approached the sanctuary, her grandmother let go of the little girl's hand and took a seat in the pew in front of me. The child, quietly and without seeking attention, began twirling in front of the altar, swishing her skirt back and forth. Then, as suddenly as she began, she stopped, curtsied, and bowed with her arms outstretched. Joining her grandmother in the pew, she wiggled in, calmly settled herself, and, with a fixed gaze, watched her granny read from an old worn prayer book.

After a few minutes, I tapped this precious child on the shoulder. Turning, she smiled. "I just want to tell you," I said, "that you look *very* cheery."

"Thank you," she endearingly replied. "I dressed up for Jesus."

This tender moment challenged me to ask what my heart wears when I come to worship. Perhaps my outfit is colorful but is mismatched. I want to sport compassion yet pass judgment on others; desire to don kindness but rush through life with harsh words; hope to put on humility even as I act as though I am the source of all my gifts; long to model quiet strength and discipline but indulge every personal whim and desire; pray to be clothed in love even as I control and manipulate my family and workplace.

Yet faith assures me that Christ takes me as I am with all my weaknesses, contradictions, and failures; adorns me with gentle acceptance; and wraps me in loving forgiveness. Once I truly believe this, my heart is set free and, in confidence and peace, I come before my Savior. Then, redeemed and dressed up for Jesus, my heart offers him a grateful and joyful twirl.

Owning the Story, Opening to Grace

■ Once, during a challenging time, God robed me in grace . . .

■ I want to clothe myself in the likeness of Christ by . . .

■ A virtue I would like to wear more often is . . .

GOD, WHO ROBES ME WITH GRACE, I come before you in confidence and in petition. Inspire me to clothe myself in virtue "and dress in the wardrobe you picked out for me: compassion, kindness, humility, quiet strength, discipline. And regardless of what else I put on, may I wear love. Grant that it may be my basic, all-purpose garment. May I never be without it" (Col. 3:12, 14, adapted from THE MESSAGE).

Clothe yourselves with the new self, created according to the likeness of God in true righteousness and holiness.

(Eph. 4:24)

37

Salt and Pepper
Service

SISTER JOANNE BASTIEN'S SIXTY YEARS AS A Maryknoll Sister, a group of Roman Catholic nuns dedicated to missionary life, reads like a best seller. But, as I turned the pages of her life in awe, Sister laughed, taking the broad sweeps all in stride.

Her ministry as a missionary began in Ceylon (now Sri Lanka). Sister Joanne studied the language, prepared herself as a nurse to serve in a hillside government hospital, was suddenly expelled after one year due to political unrest, and, undaunted, took a boat to Hong Kong. "It was not easy to start over in another country," she said.

In Hong Kong, Sister Joanne again began language studies while she worked in two clinics, treating refugees from China. "I also did health checks in two schools and then, late in the evening, would walk up seven flights of stairs. There were no elevators, you know. It was ordinary work but we all became family," she commented, her voice filled with love for these displaced people.

Although according to her religious rule she was to remain abroad for ten years, Sister Joanne was given the surprise of an unexpected family visit in the United States to celebrate her brother's ordination to the priesthood. She had no idea this short leave would have life-changing consequences. "You never know what will come next," she mused with her trademark radiant smile.

After all the parish and family festivities, she was eagerly awaiting her return to Hong Kong. As she packed her suitcase with anticipation and treasured memories with gratitude, a twist of both fate and her back sent a searing pain reeling through her spinal cord. The resulting back injury required surgery and weeks of rehabilitation. She would never again return either to Hong Kong or to foreign missionary work.

Additional medical challenges began to creep into Sister Joanne's life: a brain aneurism, pacemaker implant, mental confusion, bouts of depression, and problems with balance. But once again, she carried on in the midst of these trials, including years in Chicago's Chinatown working in the library, tutoring young boys in English, starting a Girl Scout troop, and teaching origami to fourth graders.

The next twenty years she helped care for the elderly sisters in the Maryknoll Sisters' Retirement Center in Ossining, New York. Chuckling, Sister Joanne mentioned that she taught the sisters how to make handcrafted paper gifts of snow sleds, assorted bird houses, vibrant flowers, white peace cranes, and all sorts of Halloween pumpkins and ghosts. "But I steered clear of coffins and skeletons!"

It was there at the center where I first saw Sister Joanne, her beaming serenity catching my attention. Gracefully and calmly, she walked into the dining room, cautiously carrying a tray. Assuming it held her lunch plate, I motioned to her to come to our table and join us. As she approached, I realized the tray held salt and pepper shakers.

"This is my work now," she said in the middle of her final chapter. "I'll soon be eighty-one years old, you know. It's a good job filling fifty salt and pepper shakers every other day. Just a dash can change bland to tasty. Like zest in life."

Curious as to how Sister Joanne made sense of the twist and turns of her life from dangerous foreign service, a voyage across the seas, rural nursing, physical and mental setbacks, Girl Scouts, English for refugees, elementary school origami, handicrafts with the elderly, to distributing table seasonings, I asked her the secret to an integrated life.

"Well," Sister Joanne slowly responded, "I try to live what my mother taught me over the years. Be faithful in love from generation to generation. Don't get too excited when things don't work out. Do what you can. Sometimes you'll get praise, sometimes not. Always think before you rush into things. And, most of all, don't have any problems with God when hard times come along. He's fine and you'll be too. So smile." She stood and reminded me that she had work to do. Bearing her tray like a royal servant in the court of a king, she continued her rounds.

There, I thought, *goes the salt of the earth.*

Owning the Story, Opening to Grace

■ I believe that the secret to an integrated life is . . .

■ One time when I realized that little things can make a difference and add zest to life was . . .

■ This week I will add extra love and a smile to . . .

O GOD WHO ASKS ME TO SERVE WITH ZEAL AND A SMILE, may I:

Measure heroic generosity in fidelity to my daily routine.

Practice selfless service to my family, friends, neighbors, and those who try my patience.

Remain loyal to my spiritual commitment to reflect and pray.

Conduct myself with a positive disposition when things do not go my way.

Laugh reverently in hard times, knowing it is you who will make all things right.

Live as salt of the earth, adding enthusiasm and gusto to life.

I pray this through the intercession of Maryknoll foundress, Mother Mary Joseph Rogers, a valiant woman and missionary to the world. Amen.

I would have a Maryknoll Sister distinguished by Christ-like selflessness, gracious courtesy, and the saving grace of a sense of humor.

(Mother Mary Joseph Rogers)

38

Sand Through Her Fingers
Empowerment

WAITING FOR THE FISHERMEN TO RETURN, nets heavy with the day's catch, Mariana and I sat together on the ocean shore in Dakar, Senegal. We were reminiscing and laughing about our behavior a few months earlier. After weeks of drought, I had reveled with outstretched arms in a downpour and she had danced among the mango trees in the pelting torrents.

Suddenly, I noticed that a few rays of the setting sun glistened just like raindrops on the African jade necklace she always wore. Distracted by the beauty and charm of the smooth, deep green oval beads, I abruptly interrupted our spirited conversation.

"Your necklace is exquisite, Mariana. It's dancing in the fading sunlight."

Immediately unclasping it, she offered it to me. When I embarrassingly returned the necklace, she, with noticeable hesitation, refastened it around her neck, and then scooped up a handful of sand.

"This," Mariana said, as her necklace shone in brilliance and the sand trickled through her open fingers, "is how I try to live."

When we can let go of what we have, at a moment's notice, for another's need or simple pleasure, we are set free. Every possession, material or spiritual, loses its ability to enslave or bind us. Appreciating everything but clinging to nothing, we live peacefully knowing that only God can satisfy the restless and sometimes daunting longings of our hearts. As we empty ourselves more and more as Christ emptied himself, we grasp nothing in life in tightly closed fists. We are able to surrender everything, letting it flow like sand through our fingers. As it piles up beneath our feet on the shore of life, we sink our toes into this sand with wiggles and smiles. Breathing in the fresh air of freedom, we lean back and watch our unencumbered spirit drift like clouds in the sky. As the gentle waves of our evening tide wash the shore, we hear the rhythmic chant that "all things are passing." But we are confident and at peace, for God alone suffices.

Owning the Story, Opening to Grace

- One thing I hold on tightly to in life is . . .
- My secret to letting life flow through my fingers like sand is . . .
- God alone suffices when . . .

CHRIST, YOU WHO EMPTIED YOURSELF AND CLUNG TO NOTHING, etch these words into my being, for you are all I need.

"Let nothing disturb you,
Let nothing frighten you.
All things are passing;
God never changes.
Patience attains all things.
One who has God lacks nothing:
God alone suffices." (Teresa of Avila)

"" *He who makes rich is made poor; he takes on the poverty of my flesh, that I may gain the riches of his divinity. He who is full is made empty that I may share in his fullness and power.* ""

(Gregory Nazianzen)

39

Sharing a Biscuit
Bread of Life

FOUR-YEAR-OLD ROBELAI'S FATHER, APPEARING far older than his forty years, carried his starving child into our Sudan feeding center. His feet bled with miles of walking over the barren, scorching desert. Robelai's stomach was distended, as is the case with children of famine, and we

A Story

wondered if we could ever nurse her back to health. After several weeks, Robelai put her finger in the bowl of porridge and licked it profusely. It was then that we realized hope was on the horizon. Soon she began to sit up unassisted, though wobbly and uncertain. Robelai had turned a corner toward a normal life.

One hot, sultry morning, certain that it would make it easier for Robelai to eat it, I broke a high-energy biscuit in half and handed it to her. She took one half and then, faintly smiling, tipped slightly over and put her other half in front of Ibrahim, the child next to her. Ibrahim slowly picked it up and began to eat it. Strangers to each other, they were now bonded as brother and sister and nourished together by sharing a biscuit.

We may not be children of famine, but all of us know the hunger of gnawing spiritual cravings. Wondering if we are loved, we yearn for someone's special attention and devotion. Feeling malnourished in the desert of workplace power, personal prestige, and financial success, we muse about our life's meaning and the value of our strenuous efforts. We crave the satisfaction of knowing without a shadow of doubt that we make a difference in the world around us and beyond us.

Christ, the Bread of Life, invites us to bring our hungers to him. Knowing all that we desire, he waits to feed us, to satisfy our longings, to nourish and strengthen us for what lies ahead. With blessed assurance, we can count on Christ to do more than share a biscuit with us. He gives us himself, "the true Bread come down from heaven that gives life to the world" (adapted from John 6:33). In faith may we feast at his feet, find our hungers alleviated, and then rise up to break bread with our neighbor.

Owning the Story, Opening to Grace

- I spiritually yearn for . . .
- I can reach out and nourish a hungry neighbor by . . .
- A time that my faith fed me was . . .

JESUS, BREAD OF LIFE, GRACIOUSLY FEED ME SO THAT:

My life may be a table of welcome and feast for all.

The poor may experience your divine care through my acts of giving.

Those who hunger for acceptance and understanding may hear my comforting words.

I may sacrifice myself for the lonely, abandoned, and depressed.

In sharing bread with the hungry, I may be nourished to live fruitfully and abundantly.

Amen.

Often I just stay simply seated before the Bread of Life. This calm unconscious repose does me good. I am fed; I am nourished; my strength returns so as to give to others.

(Edward Poppe)

40

Sign on the Door
Humility

KNOCKING AND BURSTING IN WITH EXCITEMENT, I flopped down onto the straight-back chair in the small room and, gushing breathlessly, rattled off the news of the day: word had just come that I was chosen as the New Orleans Junior Chamber of Commerce's Young Teacher of the Year. Being my first honor in seven years of primary teaching, I hurried to share it with Sister Elisabeth Marie, one of my favorite sisters in my religious community. Sister, a recipient of many awards and accolades herself as a first-rate musician, had retired after five and a half decades of teaching and now spent her time encouraging the rest of us.

Sister Elisabeth Marie, comfortable in her overstuffed armchair, listened to me with utter attention and intensity, convincing me that she felt my personal joy as her own. As I recounted details of the future ceremony, she chuckled, smiled, and nodded her head. She knew getting a word in edgewise was impossible, given my unrestrained enthusiasm and run-on sentences.

Dashing to the finish line of my report, I asked, "So, Sister, what do you think about all this?"

"Top-notch!" she replied. "But, before you go, I am wondering if you would do me a favor?"

"Name it," I said, ready to conquer the world for her.

"Please open my closet and read me the sign that's taped inside. It always helps me to remember what really matters."

My curiosity was piqued as I gingerly turned the knob. There on the door was a large piece of yellowed, crinkled construction paper with eleven words printed in blue markers: *I am who I am before God, no more, no less.*

I softly read them aloud, said nothing, and gently closed the closet door. Sister Elisabeth Marie whispered in humble commentary, "That's life's reality check."

Then she laughed, hugged me for all she was worth, patted me on the shoulder, and exclaimed, "Congratulations, my dear Sister, you've done our school proud."

Owning the Story, Opening to Grace

▪ When I think of who I am before God, I feel . . .

▪ Knowing who I am before God can help me keep life in perspective when . . .

▪ When I am slighted or misunderstood I find strength in . . .

O GOD, YOU WHO KNOW ME THROUGH AND THROUGH, teach me ever more who I am before you, for you have wonderfully created me and lovingly understand all my ways. In humility I pray:

"Investigate my life;

Get all the facts firsthand.

I'm an open book to you;

even from a distance, you know what I am thinking.

You know when I leave and when I get back;

I'm never out of your sight.

You know everything I'm going to say

before I start the first sentence.

I look behind me and you're there,

then up ahead and you're there, too—

your reassuring presence, coming and going.

This is too much, too wonderful.

Oh yes, you shaped me first inside, then out;

you formed me in my mother's womb. . . .

Body and soul, I am marvelously made!

I worship in adoration—what a creation!"

(Ps. 139:1–6, 13–14, THE MESSAGE)

Before God we know who we are. If we are blamed we will not be discouraged. If they call us a saint we will not put ourselves on a pedestal.

(Mother Teresa of Calcutta)

41

Slice of Life
Adversity

M R. JOSIAH AARON DOLMANN'S SPIRIT SOARS beyond the confines of his wheelchair. I first met him when he came to have his chair adjusted at The Boston Home, a long-term care facility for adults living with degenerative neurological diseases. Mr. Dolmann lives independently and with a smile illuminating his face. There is no sign of struggle with the events of his life or with his God.

After the initial pleasantries that strangers exchange, Mr. Dolmann began. "I had a test in life and now can give my testimony. Want to hear it?"

I nodded with a double dose of curiosity. He declared without fanfare that his life changed with a random bullet. At the time he was a twenty-year-old college student and decided to take a walk in the cool of an October evening. Overflowing with biology data for the next day's exam, his head screamed for fresh air. He ambled along, gaining textbook freedom with each measured, refreshing breath. He passed the neighborhood convenience store and thought about stopping for a cup of hot coffee but decided against it since study time was at a premium. Suddenly, hearing police sirens and patrol cars approaching, he realized that a robbery was in progress in this very store. He quickened his step but was not fast enough. In making his getaway, one of the three robbers shot once into the street. That bullet struck Mr. Dolmann's back and paralyzed him for these thirty-one years.

"Tell you something," he continued. "Getting up in the morning, that's the cake. So I enjoy this day's slice of life! Anything else that may happen is only icing, but sometimes the divine Baker forgets the sugar!" His booming laugh reverberated through the hall. Then, with a twinkle and a wink, he answered my unasked question. "Sure did. I passed that biology test eight months later and, almost six and a half years to the date, hung my college diploma over my dining room table."

Owning the Story, Opening to Grace

- What gets me up in the morning is . . .
- The best part of my slice of life is . . .
- God's grace enables me to accept the challenge of . . .

O DIVINE BAKER, you offer me a slice of life each morning. Fill my heart and mind with your grace to accept all of life with hope, patience, and without reserve. I know that I will not be delivered from its troubles and adversities, but I implore you to give me the strength I need to bear them. Encourage me to put all my trust in you, especially when life seems bitter and tasteless. Teach me to enjoy and savor the cake of each new day and find sweetness in my slice of life, iced with your gentle care and gracious providence. Amen.

"Do not be held back by troubles, doubts or fears, Say 'yes' each day with courage and without reserve."

(Pope John Paul II)

42

Spring Measurements
Re-creation

A S SOON AS I SAW THIRD GRADER ALICE bolt into the learning center with her pink plastic ruler, hand-decorated notebook covered with flower stickers, and flashing smile, I knew the spring ritual had begun. Each year, when the snow melts and tiny daffodil shoots wiggle their nose-tips through the softened ground, Alice begins growth measurements in her "daffodil patch" at home.

Every eye is fixed on the dry erase board as Alice carefully sketches the "more or less" size of the daffodil shoots. As she daily plots the sprouting on the graph growth chart, she assures her friends, "We just gotta wait." Using her pink ruler as a baton, Alice concludes her gardener's presentation with a rendition of an old hymn, to which she has added a new verse: "He's Got the Whole Growin' in His Hands." Clapping ends with three classroom cheers meant for divine encouragement.

As the markings heighten on the growth chart, we begin to anticipate the surprise arrival of a bright yellow bouquet. On *that* morning Alice races in, balancing her backpack and a bunch of the long-awaited daffodils. Some are still awakening from their winter sleep; other nodding and dancing in newfound freedom; still others barely surviving the squeeze of small hands. Turning to the class, Alice waves her sun-kissed bouquet and announces with utter delight, "God did it again! He put spring back in business!"

God never tires of making all things new.

Owning the Story, Opening to Grace

▪ Something inside me that I thought was dead but came back to life is . . .

▪ God gives me a treat each springtime when . . .

▪ My heart brims with gratitude when nature . . .

O FULL OF LIFE, DO-IT-AGAIN GOD,

For gentle dawns and fiery sunsets, for sparkling light on crystal streams and unexpected downpours, I praise and thank you, Surprising God.

For puppy licks and purring kittens, for toiling ants and slow-paced inchworms, I praise and thank you, Caring God.

For full moons and starry nights, for meteor showers and the Milky Way, I praise and thank you, Creator God.

For fragrant lilacs and hearty pansies, for stubborn dandelions and weeping willows, I praise and thank you, Do-It-Again God.

For fire's radiant light and precious water, for gentle wind and harvest-producing soil, I praise and thank you, Life-Giving God.

I pray, O God, that each season, each day, each moment, remind me that your heart rejoices when mine blossoms with awe and gratitude for the beauties of nature and for the times you do it again. You never fail to make all things new. Amen.

Look at those who are full of life; they love repetition. Because God is full of life, I imagine that each springtime Almighty God says to the flowers, 'Do it again.' When they do, the heart of God once more rings out.

(Fulton J. Sheen)

43

Strawberries and Champagne
Gratitude

ONE DISMAL FEBRUARY MORNING IN HER SECOND year of college, Anna Bella was unable to get up out of bed. Her strength was exhausted, her appetite gone, her tingling legs felt like wet noodles. Thinking she was getting the flu, she decided to rest in bed but would do some speed-reading for her upcoming research paper. She noticed, as she read, that the words were blurred but attributed that to the "bug" going around. Her symptoms continued, and seven months later Anna Bella was diagnosed with multiple sclerosis. She cried her way through her third-year fall semester and left college shortly after the extended Christmas break.

Four years later, Anna Bella returned to college, taking one course at a time. She earned her liberal arts degree after six years of steady studies and, shortly after receiving her diploma, married Roland, both the love of her life and a Robert Frost scholar. Her face lighting up, she reminisced how, on snowy evenings in their cabin in the New Hampshire woods, they would sip sparkling cider and share their "promises to keep and the miles to go before they sleep." Unable to have their own children, they adopted Pablo and Miguel, siblings from Central

America. The years flew by; the children grew into fine young men; and multiple sclerosis symptoms seemed to be at bay.

Suddenly one evening family life changed forever. Driving home from their college art classes, Pablo and Miguel were crossing an intersection when a drunk driver careened through a red light, slammed into their Chevy, and killed both of them instantly. Anna Bella and Roland plummeted into depression and unbearable grief. For Roland the pain was too much to bear, and he resigned his teaching position, left his wife and home, and moved across country in search of "roads not taken." For Anna Bella, multiple sclerosis reared its painful head yet another time, and her health deteriorated rapidly. She realized she could no longer live independently and moved into a nursing home. Her adjustment was slow and painful. But life finally seemed to be leveling off until a routine physical examination revealed that Anna Bella had terminal cancer.

Sitting at her bedside four months later, I wondered how one person could endure such a raw and tragic life. She had one dying wish. "I would just love some strawberries and champagne before I die," she said. "Think it's possible?"

"You'll have them tomorrow," I promised.

The next day her three favorite nurses and I gathered around her bed. "Ta da!" exclaimed Magdalena as she produced a decorative dish with tiny cut-up pieces of strawberries and a yellow plastic cup filled with champagne and tipped off with a blue-striped straw. As Magdalena bent over her bed and offered the cup of champagne, Anna Bella whispered with love and conviction, "I want to toast God for the wonderful life I have had. I promise to thank him in person." Five days later, as the full moon glistened on the snow, Anna Bella did just that.

Owning the Story, Opening to Grace

- My dying wish will be . . .
- Even in the midst of difficult times, I once managed to find the blessings of . . .
- The challenges that became spiritual gifts are . . .

BENEFICENT GOD, teach me to turn my whole life into one great act of thanksgiving. Open my heart and my eyes to be grateful for full moons on winter nights, quiet evenings with family, the beauty and wisdom of poetry, the kind and caring gesture, the wonder of a child. Do not let me miss the daily favors and graces that you shower upon me. And may I always have my strawberries and champagne at the ready to toast you, my God, who fills my life with gifts and blessings. Amen.

If the only prayer you say in your life is 'thank you,' that would suffice.

(Meister Eckhart)

44

Street Adoration
Eucharistic Presence

MY FRIEND ED CASEY, THE CHIEF FINANCIAL officer of a well-known firm, makes his way very early every morning without fail, through snowstorms, howling winds, or summer heat waves, to one of two perpetual (24/7) adoration shrines: St. Clement's in the metropolitan Boston area or Holy Ghost Church in Whitman, Massachusetts. Surrendering his day and its various business deadlines and time crunches, he lets time evaporate as he kneels in quiet prayer.

Believing in this Christ-presence opens Ed's eyes to see Jesus throughout his day in his ordinary encounters: in the hardworking counter clerks and servers at coffee shops and restaurants, the discouraged poor and ill whom he often meets, and the lonely elderly. But Ed does more than honor these faces of the divine: an overly generous tip, food and money, flowers, running errands, and spending time with others to comfort them transform his daily church adoration into action.

One day Ed shared that a request for more participants had gone out at both the adoration shrines to cover those hours when no one would be present. It was barely filled, and Ed just shook his head in disbelief. Then he quietly reflected, "If worldwide network news interrupted all broadcasts to report that Jesus

Christ was seen going into one of these adoration shrines, the most powerful people would be pushing, shoving, and using their influence to get in. Stock markets would close. People would be expecting the final judgment, creating a mob scene at the church door. But we believe that Christ *is* here.

"Why don't people cut their lunch hour short one day a week or watch television or sleep one less hour and use that time in prayer before the Blessed Sacrament? We all have twenty-four hours each day, and we all decide how to spend them. What better way is there than one hour in quiet reflection and adoration before the presence of Christ upon this earth?"

I could not resist smiling at Ed's vivid, animated musings, but, deep down, I knew he was right.

In Eucharistic adoration, Jesus bids us to come into his presence in confidence and peace. In surrender and in need, we can approach our Blessed Savior just as we are. Our senses may fail us, but unwavering faith tells us that Christ is truly before us, present both in his humanity and in his divinity. As we adore Christ in reverent silence, he bids us rise from our knees, extend our church prayer to bustling city streets, and honor him everywhere.

Owning the Story, Opening to Grace

■ I witness to Christ's presence among us when . . .

■ My prayer flows into action when . . .

■ In trust and confidence, I ask for the Eucharistic grace this week to . . .

O CHRIST, TRULY PRESENT IN THE EUCHARIST AND ON THE STREETS, "you are with me today and you continue to need me. You need my eyes to continue to see. You need my strength to continue to work and my voice to continue to teach. You need my hands to continue to bless and my heart to continue to love. You need my whole being to build up your Body. As I believe, so let me live" (Joseph Bernardin).

"*When I am before the Blessed Sacrament I feel such a lively faith that I can't describe it. Christ in the Eucharist is almost tangible to me. When it is time for me to leave, I have to tear myself away from his sacred presence.*"

(Anthony Mary Claret)

45

Talk and Truth
Experience

THE LARGE AUDITORIUM WAS PACKED WITH people sitting on the edge of their seats. The trained orator and Broadway actor approached the podium. A recipient of many drama and speech awards, Professor Alphonse Lange was poised to recite the Twenty-third Psalm. After one slow, deep breath, his melodious voice filled the room: "The Lord is my Shepherd; I shall not want." His perfect pauses, accompanying hand gestures, and powerful verbal stresses brought the psalmist's words to life. When Professor Lange finished, the audience rose to its feet and gave him a standing ovation with shouts of "encore, encore!"

Professor Lange bowed graciously and then asked his friend Pastor Calvin Rochester to come forward. Hesitantly climbing the three steps to the stage, this elderly man limped unsteadily toward the Professor. Extending his hand in assistance and welcome, Professor Lange introduced him to the audience.

"Reverend Calvin has walked through dark valleys of pain and suffering, his own as well as those of the congregation he has faithfully served for forty-one years. In the midst of every trial, he has restored his soul in the restful waters of prayer, followed the path of righteousness in spite of personal misunderstanding, found comfort leaning on the heart of God, and been grateful for all the blessings flowing from the cup of his life."

Professor Lange paused in personal admiration and then asked, "Reverend Rochester, would you do us the honor of accepting my encore?"

The humble pastor wobbled to the microphone. Without a deep breath or dramatic hand gestures, his raspy words came forth: "The Lord is my Shepherd. I shall not want." When he finished, a stunned silence fell over the listeners. No one applauded; no one jumped in elation; no one called for an encore. Pastor Rochester haltingly descended the stage and took his seat.

Professor Lange returned to the podium. He eyed the elderly man and confessed to the audience, "The difference between what you heard from me and what you heard from Reverend Rochester is the difference between talk and truth. I know the psalm; my friend knows the Shepherd."

Owning the Story, Opening to Grace

▪ My prayers come alive when I . . .
▪ What I know about the Good Shepherd is . . .
▪ I make the Twenty-third Psalm a reality when . . .

GOD, MY SHEPHERD!

I don't need a thing.
You have bedded me down in lush meadows,
you find me quiet pools to drink from.
True to your word,
you let me catch my breath
and send me in the right direction.
Even when the way goes through
Death Valley,
I'm not afraid
when you walk at my side.
Your trusty shepherd's crook
makes me feel secure.
You serve me a six-course dinner
right in front of my enemies.
You revive my drooping head;
my cup brims with blessing.
Your beauty and love chase after me
every day of my life.
I'm back home in the house of God
for the rest of my life.
(Ps. 23, THE MESSAGE)

'I am the good shepherd. I know my own and my own know me, just as the Father knows me and I know the Father.'
(John 10:14–15)

46

Tender Moment
Nurturing

M Y FIRST GRADERS WERE ON COUNTDOWN till Christmas. After our lesson on Christ's birth, I asked them to draw a picture of what's happening in the stable in Bethlehem.

About twenty minutes later, Andrew bounded up with his paper. "Mary and Joseph are *sooo* happy. Here's my picture!"

Andrew's paper was framed with thick, brown-colored lines that represented the stable. There were a few blue and purple drums scattered around the floor, beside which lay one dog, two cats, and a sheep. In the upper center was an orange star with rays emanating onto an empty manger. *Where is Jesus?* I wondered curiously.

On the far left margin of his drawing paper, he had sketched a figure of St. Joseph. On the far right margin, Mary was holding the Christ Child, who had a scarlet smile, quite out of proportion and far too developed for an infant, stretched across his face. The middle section of the construction paper had a long, skinny "arm" with five stick fingers stretching from St. Joseph and reaching Jesus in a tummy tickle. And across the bottom of the paper Andrew had printed in large red and green letters: "Gitchy, gitchy goo!"

In that tender caress Joseph may have been grateful that he listened to his dreams, did what seemed best regardless of public opinion, and went where he was asked to go. Perhaps he anticipated teaching Jesus the woodworker's trade, passing on the values of a life of hard labor, and laying the foundations of his religious faith. But none of that was important now.

What really mattered and what Andrew had captured were the wonder and the awe of a new parent. In that cold stable on that dark night, Joseph, in his fatherly love for the infant in his care, knew that the Christ Child would love what all babies love, a gentle touch that would send a tiny smile into the world.

Owning the Story, Opening to Grace

■ If I painted a picture of Christ's birth, some loving details would be . . .

■ Ways to model St. Joseph in my family might include . . .

■ I can nurture children this week by . . .

O GOOD ST. JOSEPH,

Husband of the Mother of God, pray for us.

Foster father of the Son of God, pray for us.

Faithful guardian of Christ, pray for us.

Head of the Holy Family, pray for us.

Joseph, obedient and loyal, pray for us.

Example to parents, pray for us.

Pillar of family life, pray for us.

Protector of the Church, pray for us.

I ask your intercession through the love you bore for Mary and for the Child Jesus. Amen.

(from the traditional litany of St. Joseph)

> *St. Joseph was a just man, a tireless worker, the upright guardian of those entrusted to his care. May he always guard, protect and enlighten families.*
>
> (Pope John Paul II)

47

The Long Haul
Perseverance

WITH AROMATIC WHIFFS OF GINGER AND nutmeg permeating the convent hall, eighty-six-year-old Sister Philomena peddles her culinary wares to the community and office staff. "Cinnamon spice is the cookie of the day! Take a break and come get one!" For fifty of her sixty-six years of religious life, she has been the convent cook. After these generous years of laboring in the kitchen, she revealed perseverance's secret: "To be faithful to my work, I've got to season it with daily prayer. Because prayer and fidelity always hold hands."

Sister's kitchen is a place of reflection and prayer. From the large windows one can contemplate the beauty of pink rhododendrons bursting into spring blooms, of vibrant red maples shimmering after a rain, and of snow quietly piling up on frozen ground. On a window sill, St. Joseph the Worker supervises every meal's preparation. With animated monologues, Sister Philomena calls upon him for everything: success for untried recipes and creative leftovers, help for the delivery personnel and their families, even for a winning streak for her sluggish hometown baseball team. Passing by, one feels her peace, the fruit of countless years of devotion and loving service.

Other times, a surprise visit reveals a calming silence, broken only by the rhythmic jingle of rosary beads slipping through gnarled fingers. Upon every egg she beats, every loaf of bread she bakes, every pot she washes, and every countertop she shines, Sister Philomena sprinkles prayer.

In the past few years, cooking and baking have become more difficult. Sister has had to adjust the can opener to fit her arthritic hands; a stool accommodates her swollen knees; and potatoes and carrots take longer to peel. But Sister Philomena is in it for the long haul, for she knows she is serving Christ by feeding others. Over and over she assures us, "As long as my heart pumps and my feet thump, I'll keep my oven on, my cookies baking, and my heart praying."

Owning the Story, Opening to Grace

- ■ I find strength for persevering in my work by . . .
- ■ The graces I need to be faithful for the long haul are . . .
- ■ I encourage others to be faithful in their commitments by . . .

GOD OF MY DAILY LABOR, may I find encouragement to persevere in my work as I pray your divine counsels.

"Well-done work is its own reward." (Prov. 12:14, THE MESSAGE)

"Don't hold back. Throw yourselves into the work of the Master, confident that nothing you do for [God] is a waste of time." (1 Cor. 15:58, THE MESSAGE)

"As long as I'm alive in this body, there is good work for me to do." (Phil. 1:22, THE MESSAGE)

"As you learn more and more how God works, you will learn how to do *your* work. We pray that you'll have the strength to stick it out over the long haul—not the grim strength of gritting your teeth but the glory-strength God gives." (Col. 1:10–12, THE MESSAGE)

"Don't just do the minimum that will get you by. Do your best. Work from the heart for your real Master, for God, confident that you'll get paid in full when you come into your inheritance. Keep in mind always that the ultimate Master you're serving is Christ." (Col. 3:22–24, THE MESSAGE)

> *We can present our souls to God in our work a thousand times a day. Sprinkle a seasoning of short prayers on your daily work. When you are in need, pray to God. When you see something beautiful, thank God for it. You can toss up many prayers all day long. Prayer will help you persevere in your work.*
>
> (Francis de Sales)

48

The Look in Her Eye
Concern

FATHER CRAIG, A DEDICATED PRIEST, WAS HAVING a hard year. As campus minister at a large state college, he faced the lethargy of students and long night hours at the Catholic Center. As a part-time parish priest, he had homilies to prepare and confessions to hear. The youngest of three priests living in the church rectory, he felt at times misunderstood and alone. Feeling overwhelmed by an increasing workload, difficult relationships, and additional commitments, his confidence waned. "It was a dismal time. So to gather my wits and find some peace, I did what a son would do. I called my mother!" he told me with a chuckle in his voice.

Father Craig poured out his heart to his mother over the phone. In her maternal wisdom she realized that only he could solve his problems. But she listened intently and occasionally offered a word or two. Father Craig thanked her but hung up wondering if his mother *really* understood.

The following Sunday, as Father Craig was giving his homily at Mass, he looked up from his notes and, lo and behold, there was his dear mother sitting in the front pew. Her eyes were fixed on him in an empathetic gaze; her face lit up in a caring smile. Though distracted by her surprise visit, he felt healing energy seeping through his veins.

Hugging his mother after Mass, he asked her in disbelief, "Mom, I can't believe you traveled fifty-two miles in the pouring rain just to come to my Mass. Your arthritic knees certainly must have been tested by such a long trip. Why on earth did you come?"

Edna quietly replied, "After your phone call, Craig, I just wanted you to look out and see someone who loves you."

Father Craig knew his troubles would not dissolve with his mother's presence. But her surprise visit reminded this young priest that God always accompanies him in each stressful situation, accepts him with admiration and concern, and cherishes him as a beloved son. In his mother's look through her thick bifocals, Father Craig saw a reflection of God's encouraging gaze filled with unconditional love.

Owning the Story, Opening to Grace

- I once offered the gift of a loving gaze when I . . .
- I reflect God's acceptance and understanding by . . .
- Like a loving parent, I show care and concern when . . .

GOD OF LOVING GAZES, GRANT THAT I MAY:

Notice when another desires the gift of an understanding look.

Perceive when others need encouragement to replace discouragement.

See and act when friends are lonely and walking without hope.

Note when someone, troubled and anxious, wants peace.

Behold your divine care in all aspects of life.

Sing because your eye is upon me setting me free.

Whenever I am tempted, whenever clouds arise,
When songs give place to sighing, when hope within me dies,
I draw the closer to him, from care he sets me free;
His eye is on the sparrow and I know he watches me.
His eye is on the sparrow, and I know he watches me.
("His Eye Is on the Sparrow," traditional hymn)

49

Up in the Air
Faith

T WAS A LONG FLIGHT FROM ST. LOUIS TO San Francisco. For me it was not just a question of the four-plus hours of travel but also managing the fear I have of flying and the constant anticipation of turbulence.

Seated next to me was a minister from rural Kentucky, Reverend Silas Wildes, both a southern gentleman and a man of God, who was headed to an evangelical conference in the San Francisco Bay area. Quickly discovering our common bond, we passed most of the time sharing about God's daily providential care for us, the unwavering faith that we need to permeate our life, and the call to deepen our relationship with Jesus beyond the laws of our particular religious affiliations. Although we revealed pieces of our heart, I kept my fear of flying to myself.

Breathing with relief at the relatively smooth flight and checking my watch for the time left until we landed, I cringed when I heard the pilot's voice. In a somber tone he asked the flight attendants to take their seats and the passengers to fasten their seat belts. He added that the control tower had indicated a "very bumpy" descent. In reality, I knew that *really* meant significant turbulence. My heart began to pound and sweat rolled down my face. Reverend Wildes just gazed peacefully out the window as the roller coaster ride began.

After about ten minutes of choppiness, Reverend Wildes leaned over and whispered, "Well, I see the water and wonder if we are landing just a bit too close to it because I can see fish jumping and splashing." Panicking, I reached under my seat to check for my life vest and then, boldly and humbly, asked the reverend if I might hold his hand.

With a gentle smile and elegant courtesy, he extended his hand and then asked me a question I have never forgotten: "Sister, you seem to be living with so much unfaltering faith on the ground. Why then do you lose it when you are up in the air?"

Owning the Story, Opening to Grace

■ When my life seems up in the air, I can strengthen my faith by . . .

■ The times I need the outstretched, comforting hand of another are . . .

■ I can renew my trust during turbulent times by . . .

GOD OF SEA AND SKY, increase my faith when situations in life are turbulent or evoke fear in me. Help me to etch this prayer upon my heart: "There is hardly a moment when you do not approach us disguised as a challenge. If we could lift the curtain and observe what is really happening, we would see you, God, constantly at work. We would be rejoicing all the time, because 'It is the Lord.' We would accept every experience that comes our way as a gift from you. Faith identifies you at work. Faith transforms our perception. Faith is our light." (Jean-Pierre de Caussade).

> *But when [Peter] noticed the strong wind, he became frightened, and beginning to sink, he cried out, 'Lord, save me!' Jesus immediately reached out his hand and caught him, saying to him, 'You of little faith, why did you doubt?'*
>
> (Matt. 14:30–31)

50

Watching Myrtle
Prayer

"WATCH REAL GOOD HOW YOUR GRANNY PRAYS. It will be the first thing you think of when you are old and need God." Eight-year-old Ladonna's counsel sparked memories of my own grandmother.

Myrtle Tate Tangue lived as a widow for twenty years. I can still see the rosary that she kept on top of her Bible in front of

A Story

the television set. I remember how the La-Z-Boy recliner chair she called "Hon's" (her name for my deceased grandfather), often covered with his sparkling white barber towels, served as a bookshelf for her stack of prayer books. Morning and evening would find her "reading my prayers" or "praying the rosary" or "talking to Hon about heaven."

But Gram was certainly not a rote prayer factory. Her prayers spilled over into life. She would talk about the simple things: the beauty of the rose bushes outside her kitchen door; how she worried about her neighbor, "old man Faulk," in his illness; how she laughed when she found some of the money Hon stored in Band Aid boxes around the house; how much she missed my Grandpa and thought about their reunion.

As I reflect now on her musings and our conversations, I realize that, over the years of fingering her rosary and turning the pages of the hand-creamed-stained pages of her prayer books, my grandmother had become a model of wonder, gratitude, and intercession.

Thinking of my beloved Gram reminds me that, in retirement villages, assisted care facilities, and nursing homes around the world, there are hundreds of pious widows and widowers. Having spent decades attending church services and spending time in faithful devotions, these men and women, like my grandmother, have been transformed into living prayers.

Indeed, we do well to watch how they pray.

Owning the Story, Opening to Grace

▪ The prayers of wise elders teach me that . . .

▪ I can put my prayers into action by . . .

▪ This week I will pray with my infirm and fragile friends by . . .

GOD OF EVERYDAY PROPHETS, as I watch and share in the devotion and wisdom of the elders, teach me to listen without interrupting (Prov. 18:13), give without holding back (Prov. 21:26), trust without wavering (1 Cor. 13:7), act without complaining (Phil. 2:14), and speak without judging (Jas. 1:19). Form me into a living prayer to the praise of your glory. Amen.

There was also a prophet, Anna . . . of great age, having lived with her husband seven years after her marriage, then as a widow to the age of eighty-four. She never left the temple but worshiped there with fasting and prayer night and day. At that moment she came, and began to praise God and to speak about the child to all who were looking for the redemption of Jerusalem.

(Lk. 2:36–38)

51

What a Buddy!
Encouragement

A BORN LEADER, BUDDY HAD ORGANIZED the class to slam their geography books and let out a howl at exactly 10:16 AM on Halloween. A budding artist, he secretly exchanged all the magic markers in the classroom container for green crayon stubs on St. Patrick's Day. He turned his winning smile into an exaggerated pout and extended his fingers in "rabbit ears" just as the photographer snapped our class photo for the school yearbook.

Over the months, Buddy wore my patience thin, but I was convinced he had potential and possibility. Engaging in mental gymnastics, I tried to find excuses that would explain his annoying and sometimes disruptive behavior as well as devise methods to channel his talent and energy. I assured myself that my teacher's determination and efforts would make me victorious in battle.

The last day of school proved me wrong. Buddy had smuggled in two water balloons that popped and sprayed in sync with the sound of the end-of-the-year dismissal bell. All I could do was to wish him a good summer and begin fervent prayers for the seventh grade teacher.

In the years that went by, thoughts of Buddy had faded until an autumn day last year. My curiosity piqued when a "new e-mail message" notice popped up on my computer screen. Seeing the sender's name set off bells and whistles. Could this be the one and only Buddy?

"Sister, do you remember me?" his e-mail began. "I was in your sixth grade class thirty-seven years ago. The first thing I want to say is that I am sorry for some things I did, but you probably don't even recall what they were. I'm glad because that means I'm off the hook! Maybe you would be happy to know that my wife, Cindy, and I have been married for twenty-three years. We have four great kids, three girls and one boy, our youngest. Three years ago I bought the dry cleaners where I worked for seventeen years. I treat each customer with respect, turn a profit, and provide well for my family. You probably realize that I love my family, but I also want you to know that I love my faith and try to live a good life. I know I must have driven you crazy some days, but you always smiled at me and even gave me the 'big responsibility' (as you announced to the class) of taking care of our fire-bellied newt. That made me proud, but I didn't let on. I don't know how you did it, but you never, ever gave up on me. I have been grateful for that all these years.

Sincerely,

Your former student,

Buddy Callahan

P.S. I sure would appreciate any extra prayers you have for my son, Daniel. He is just like I was as a kid, if you know what I mean. He does such foolish things. But I'm hanging on."

Chuckling as I hit "reply," I thought to myself: *That's the spirit, Buddy, and that's the work of the Holy Spirit within you!*

Owning the Story, Opening to Grace

- ▪ Someone refused to give up on me when . . .
- ▪ I can accept those who annoy me by . . .
- ▪ God gave me a fresh start when . . .

O GOD OF STEADY ENCOURAGEMENT,
"you made my life complete
when I placed all the pieces before you.
When I got my act together,
you gave me a fresh start.
Now I am alert to all your ways
and never take you for granted.
Every day I review the way you work
and try to miss nothing.
I feel put back together
and I'm watching my step.
You rewrote the text of my life
when I opened the book of my heart to your eyes."
(Ps. 18:20–24, adapted from THE MESSAGE)

❝*So if anyone is in Christ, there is a new creation: every-thing old has passed away; see, everything has become new!*❞

(2 Cor. 5:17)

52

Where and What
God's Will

FOR EIGHT OF HIS FORTY-ONE YEARS, LOWELL has struggled with a mental confusion stemming from his degenerative neurological disease. Most days he propels his manual wheelchair up and down the nursing home halls, often stopping and then retracing his route. He seems as lost in the spacious corridors as he is in life.

One afternoon, Lowell seemed decidedly more befuddled than usual.

"What's up?" I asked.

Smiling pleasantly, Lowell replied, baffled, "Just tell me where to go and what to do when I get there."

"Ah," I chuckled, "How many times I wish God would do the same for me!"

How often we push through life, trying to discover the will of God. But what we most seek remains hidden and mysterious. We long to do what God wishes, yet our earnest, inquiring prayers go unanswered. We may feel we are left alone, going back and forth without purpose along our life's route.

True, we do not have the convenience of a detailed road map to find God's will in our lives. But we do have some guides to point the way: the teachings of Jesus in Sacred Scripture; the promptings of the Holy Spirit in our prayer; the wise, spiritual counsel of others along our path; and the thoughtful consideration of all options open to us. Gradually exploring each of these paths will lead us closer to where we are to go and what we are to do.

Even more, we may discover in our questing that seeking the will of God is not a task or a set of goals replete with programs or methods. What finding the divine will means is that we center our hearts on our relationship with God, seek first his kingdom, and generously respond to its challenges. Putting God first and responding to the needs around us are God's desires for us and will certainly move us in the right direction.

Owning the Story, Opening to Grace

■ I know God's desire for me when . . .

■ A time when I sought "the where and the what" of the divine plan was . . .

■ I renew my resolve this week to center my life in God by . . .

GOD OF MY DESIRE, enlighten my mind as I reflect on your Holy Word; enlighten my heart as I pray to do your holy Will.

"Trust in the Lord with all your heart,
and do not rely on your own insight.
In all your ways acknowledge him,
and he will make straight your paths." (Prov. 3:5–6)

"And when you turn to the right or when you turn to the left, your ears shall hear a word behind you, saying, 'This is the way; walk in it.'" (Isa. 30:21)

"But strive first for the kingdom of God and his righteousness, and all these things will be given to you as well." (Matt. 6:33)

"Do not be conformed to this world, but be transformed by the renewing of your minds, so that you may discern what is the will of God—what is good and acceptable and perfect." (Rom. 12:2)

"Rejoice always, pray without ceasing, give thanks in all circumstances; for this is the will of God in Christ Jesus for you." (1 Thess. 5:16–18)

"Yours I am, for You I was born:
What do You want of me?" (Teresa of Avila)

" Our salvation and perfection consist in doing the will of God, which we must have in view in all things and at every moment of our life. "

(Peter Claver)

CONCLUSION

We have opened fifty-two doors.

Some were already ajar, swinging easily on their hinges, for we are daily deepening in their virtues. One or two others needed us to jiggle the knob and push with our knee or our shoulder because the trait challenged us. Still another door required us to gain leverage and push hard against our resistance to its spiritual disposition.

What is important is that each door is open, no matter the method we used. Just opening doors, however, is not enough. Each day we are to enter slowly and thoughtfully into the rooms of our ordinary experiences. We are to notice each floor plank of the faith that supports us, every ceiling beam of the providence that protects us, and the surprise nooks and disguised crannies of God's ongoing presence. In so doing, we discover, without a shadow of a doubt, that every event in our life is gift, grace, and blessing, a door to the sacred, and a hint of the holy.

ACKNOWLEDGMENTS

It takes a team to produce a book! I would like to express my gratitude to my brother Albert Haase, OFM, who, in the midst of a busy preaching and writing schedule, always had time to offer editorial suggestions; Gay Vernon who, with a keen eye and loving heart, provided valuable input; Jon Sweeney, Bob Edmonson, Jeff Reimer, and the staff of Paraclete Press who, with attention and creativity, brought a manuscript to publication; and my Ursuline Sisters, family, and friends who, with enthusiasm and encouragement, cheered me on to the finish line.

BRIEF BIOGRAPHIES
OF THE SAINTS AND HOLY PEOPLE QUOTED IN THIS BOOK

ANGELA MERICI (1474–1540): Born at Desenzano del Garda, Lombardy, Italy, she was a Franciscan tertiary, pilgrim, teacher, and foundress of the Ursulines.

ANTHONY MARY CLARET (1807–1870): A tireless missionary and founder of the Missionary Sons of the Immaculate Heart of Mary. He was the archbishop of Santiago, Cuba, and chaplain to the queen of Spain.

AUGUSTINE OF HIPPO (354–430): The most influential theologian of his time. Born in Tagaste, North Africa, he became bishop of Hippo and is best known for his spiritual autobiography, *Confessions*.

BERNARD OF CLAIRVAUX (1090–1153): Brilliant theologian who influenced Christian mysticism and devotion to the Blessed Virgin Mary; reformer of the Cistercian Order; last of the Fathers of the church.

DAMIEN OF MOLOKAI (1840–1889): Belgian priest and member of the Congregation of the Sacred Hearts of Jesus and Mary. "The Leper Priest" ministered on the island of Molokai, Hawaii, to those who had been placed in government quarantine due to Hansen's disease.

EDWARD POPPE (1890–1924): Belgian priest. He wrote numerous texts for the "Eucharistic Crusade," and was spiritual leader of the military school in Lepoldsburg, Belgium.

FRANCIS DE SALES (1567–1622): Doctor of the Church, patron of journalists and writers. He served as bishop of Geneva and guided St. Jane Frances de Chantal in the foundation of the Order of the Visitation. He is known for his devotional guide *Introduction to the Devout Life*, the first spiritual book written exclusively for the laity.

FRANCIS OF ASSISI (1181–1226): Son of a wealthy merchant, he was a preacher and the founder of the Order of Friars Minor (Franciscans). He bore in his body the wounds of the crucified Christ (stigmata).

FULTON J. SHEEN (1895–1979): First regular speaker on NBC Radio's *Catholic Hour*; host of the television series *Life is Worth Living*; national director of the World Mission Society for the Propagation of the Faith; archbishop, acclaimed author, and international speaker.

GREGORY NAZIANZEN (C. 330–395): Doctor of the Church and also called "the Theologian" for his writings, especially on the Trinity. His father, mother, and two brothers are also saints.

IGNATIUS OF LOYOLA (1491–1556): Born to the Basque nobility in Spain, he was the founder of the Society of Jesus (Jesuits). His *Spiritual Exercises* and Ignatian method of personal prayer continue to inspire individuals in many different faiths.

JEAN-PIERRE DE CAUSSADE (1675–1751): French Jesuit priest. His classic work, *Abandonment to Divine Providence*, promotes a lifestyle of continual response to what he calls "the sacrament of the present moment."

JOHN XXIII (1881–1963): Baptized Angelo Roncalli, he was the 261st bishop of Rome (1958–1963) and convened the Second Vatican Council.

JOHN HENRY NEWMAN (1801–1890): Oratorian priest and prolific English author. A convert from Anglicanism to Roman Catholicism, he was named a cardinal by Pope Leo XIII.

JOHN PAUL II (1920–2005): Baptized Karol Wojtyla, he was the 264th bishop of Rome for twenty-seven years (1978–2005).

JOSEPH BERNARDIN (1928–1996): Born in Columbia, South Carolina. He served as auxiliary bishop of Atlanta, Georgia; first general secretary and then president of the National Conference of Catholic Bishops; archbishop of Cincinnati, Ohio, and of Chicago, Illinois. He was elevated to cardinal by Pope John Paul II.

MAHATMA (MOHANDAS) GANDHI (1869–1948): Prolific writer and leader of Indian nationalism in British-ruled India. He inspired movements for nonviolence, civil rights, and freedom across the world.

MARY JOSEPH ROGERS (1882–1955): Born Mollie Rogers. Her vision of Catholic women missionaries led to the foundation of the Maryknoll Sisters of St. Dominic.

MEISTER ECKHART (1260–C. 1329): One of the Rhineland mystics, he explored the relationship between God and human beings.

MONICA OF HIPPO (331–387): Mother of Augustine of Hippo. She led a prayerful life dedicated to the conversion of her son.

MOTHER TERESA OF CALCUTTA (1910–1997): Born Agnes Gonxha Bojaxhiu, she was foundress of the Missionaries of Charity and recipient of the Nobel Peace Prize. She gave her life to the poor and sick in the slums of India.

OSCAR ROMERO (1917–1980): Priest and advocate for the poor and human rights in El Salvador. He was assassinated as he celebrated Mass in the chapel of the hospital where he lived.

PATRICK OF IRELAND (C. 389–461): Born in Roman Britain. He is honored as the patron of Ireland and, as a wandering bishop for thirty years, worked toward the conversion of its people to Christianity.

PAULINUS OF NOLA (353–431): Roman senator and distinguished poet. His friendship with Ambrose of Milan led to his conversion and baptism in 389. He renounced his wealth and position and lived as a hermit, caring for the shrine of St. Felix of Nola.

PAUL OF THE CROSS (1694–1775): Founded, with his brother Jean Baptist, an order dedicated to preaching the passion of Christ (Passionists). He is also known for his gifts of healing, conversion of criminals, and prophecy.

PETER CLAVER (1580–1654): A Jesuit from South America, he found his mission ministering for thirty-three years to the African slaves brought to the port of Cartagena, Colombia.

PHILIP NERI (1515–1595): Founder of the Congregation of the Oratory, he preached in the streets of Rome with a joyful eccentricity, humility, and gentleness.

TERESA OF AVILA (1515–1582): Reformer of the Carmelite Order, mystic, and Doctor of the Church. Her works include her *Autobiography*, *The Way of Perfection*, and *The Interior Life*.

THOMAS À KEMPIS (1380–1471): Born in Kempen, Germany. As a monk, he copied two Bibles, each in ten volumes. *The Imitation of Christ* is ascribed to him.

THOMAS MERTON (1915–1968): Trappist monk at the Abbey of Gethsemani, Kentucky. He was one of the great spiritual writers of the twentieth century. His autobiography, *Seven Storey Mountain,* has become a classic.

VINCENT DE PAUL (1580–1660): French priest, chaplain to Queen Margaret of Valois, and founder of the Vincentians. He dedicated himself to the service of the poor and to the education of the clergy.

ABOUT PARACLETE PRESS

Who We Are

Paraclete Press is a publisher of books, recordings, and DVDs on Christian spirituality. Our publishing represents a full expression of Christian belief and practice—from Catholic to Evangelical, from Protestant to Orthodox.

We are the publishing arm of the Community of Jesus, an ecumenical monastic community in the Benedictine tradition. As such, we are uniquely positioned in the marketplace without connection to a large corporation and with informal relationships to many branches and denominations of faith.

What We Are Doing

BOOKS Paraclete publishes books that show the richness and depth of what it means to be Christian. Although Benedictine spirituality is at the heart of all that we do, we publish books that reflect the Christian experience across many cultures, time periods, and houses of worship. We publish books that nourish the vibrant life of the church and its people—books about spiritual practice, formation, history, ideas, and customs.

We have several different series, including the best-selling Paraclete Essentials and Paraclete Giants series of classic texts in contemporary English; Voices from the Monastery—men and women monastics writing about living a spiritual life today; award-winning poetry; best-selling gift books for children on the occasions of baptism and first communion; and the Active Prayer Series that brings creativity and liveliness to any life of prayer.

RECORDINGS From Gregorian chant to contemporary American choral works, our music recordings celebrate sacred choral music through the centuries. Paraclete distributes the recordings of the internationally acclaimed choir Gloriæ Dei Cantores, praised for their "rapt and fathomless spiritual intensity" by *American Record Guide,* and the Gloriæ Dei Cantores Schola, which specializes in the study and performance of Gregorian chant. Paraclete is also the exclusive North American distributor of the recordings of the Monastic Choir of St. Peter's Abbey in Solesmes, France, long considered to be a leading authority on Gregorian chant.

VIDEOS Our videos offer spiritual help, healing, and biblical guidance for life issues: grief and loss, marriage, forgiveness, anger management, facing death, and spiritual formation.

Learn more about us at our website:
www.paracletepress.com,
  or call us toll-free at 1-800-451-5006.

SCAN TO
READ
MORE

YOU MAY ALSO BE INTERESTED IN

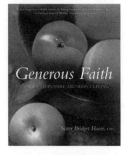

Generous Faith

SISTER BRIDGET HAASE, OSU
ISBN: 978-1-55725-615-7
$16.99 Paperback

EXPERIENCE THE GENEROSITY OF GOD in this very moment, live in the now, trust, and experience God's presence in your life. This simple and joy-filled book opens our hearts to what is in the air we breathe, under our feet, and in this very moment: the abundant life, a gift from God. This is a collection of stories that give shape and face to living in the moment, trusting in Divine care and experiencing God's presence.

"In addition to sharing powerful stories of seemingly ordinary experiences, Sister wisely directs us to take the time to ponder, reflect, and be attentive to the ways the Lord is working on our lives. We all need to make time and space for God if we want to understand our calling and our mission...." —Cardinal Sean O'Malley, Archbishop of Boston

Life Is a Gift

PARACLETE PRESS
ISBN: 978-1-61261-412-0
$16.99, Hardcover

THIS BEAUTIFUL BOOK CHALLENGES people to live in a way that blesses God, from whom all good things come. The person who goes through life being thankful for God's gifts and blessings usually experiences more of life's goodness—and inhabits more of God's blessings. Reflections from a wide array of authors are included: Henry van Dyke, Abraham Lincoln, and Louisa May Alcott, as well as many songs, psalms, and prayers.

AVAILABLE FROM MOST BOOKSELLERS OR THROUGH PARACLETE PRESS:
www.paracletepress.com
1-800-451-5006
Try your local bookstore first.